A Reader's Guide to
Rilke's *Sonnets to Orpheus*

ARLEN ACADEMIC

The Austrian Anschluss in History and Literature
Eoin Bourke

James Liddy: A Critical Study
Brian Arkins

A Reader's Guide to Rilke's *Sonnets to Orpheus*
Timothy J. Casey

Conserving the Emerald Tiger:
The Politics of Environmental Regulation in Ireland
George Taylor

Exploring John's Gospel:
Reading, Interpretation and Knowledge
Colm Luibheid

Nineteenth-Century Ireland Through German Eyes
Eoin Bourke

A Reader's Guide to
Rilke's *Sonnets to Orpheus*

Timothy J. Casey

Arlen House
2001

© Timothy J. Casey 2001

All rights reserved.

First published in March 2001

Published by Arlen House
PO Box 222
Galway
Ireland

and

42 Grange Abbey Road
Baldoyle
Dublin 13

ISBN 1-903631-09-2, paperback
ISBN 1-903631-10-6, hardback

www.arlenhouse.ie

Cover design by Dunleavy Design, Salthill, Galway
Typesetting: Arlen House
Printed by: ColourBooks, Baldoyle Industrial Estate, Dublin 13.

Contents:

Acknowledgements	xi
Preface	1
Rilke's Life and Work	5
Orpheus. Eurydike. Hermes	41
Duino Elegies	53
The *Sonnets to Orpheus*	63

to Erika

Acknowledgements

Ever since my postgraduate years in University College Dublin, whatever else in German literature I concentrated on from time to time, Rilke has probably been my most constant interest. Hence, if I were to acknowledge those who have helped me with this Rilke study, it would be a long roll-call of colleagues over many years. I make do here with mentioning the first and the last. The first and decisive debt was to the enthusiastic teaching of Professor Mary Macken of UCD, who led me away – a narrow escape – from a life of law to a life of literature. (With hindsight, given the gauche *Unschuld vom Lande* she was faced with, I can only marvel at her patience and persistence). After that, a succession of teachers, examiners and then colleagues, in Ireland, in Germany and in the United Kingdom, with their encouragement, inspiration and friendship. Finally I am deeply grateful to my colleagues here in Galway who made the publication of this book their concern, to Professor Eoin Bourke, Dr Ricca Edmondson, Professor Colm Luibhéid and Professor Markus Wórner. And to the University and President Ó Muircheartaigh who so generously responded.

This Rilke study developed out of one of those UCG interdisciplinary series of lectures, in which, in this particular case, one was faced with the challenge of introducing a major work of German literature to students, few of whom were students of German and some of whom were not primarily students of literature, but of some other branch of the humanities. I should like this work to be regarded as thanks, after so many good years there, to Galway University.

A Reader's Guide to
Rilke's *Sonnets to Orpheus*

Preface

In the library of literature about Rilke since the 1920s the *Duino Elegies* take up the most room, at any rate for those who favour the later Rilke and *vis-à-vis* the *Sonnets*, which are seen as a by-product of the central elegiac experience. It is true that some of the most perceptive and influential Rilke critics – Mason would be a notable example[1] – seem to favour the *Sonnets* as a matter of personal preference, just as they have misgivings about the *Elegies*, or at least about the purported "ideas" of the *Elegies*. But the *Elegies* continue to dominate the thinking on Rilke, in one sense rightly so, for the Duino experience remains the central fact and fundament of Rilke's life and work. It takes one a long time fully to appreciate the *Sonnets*, not so much their artistry, for that is immediately evident, but their significance as being, more even than the *Elegies*, the single most comprehensive and convincing poetic correlative of Rilke's life-experience, his feelings, values, beliefs.

This is a reader's guide, not an exhaustive line-by-line and word-by-word critical commentary in the manner, say, of Mörchen on the *Sonnets* or Steiner on the *Elegies*.[2] As reference works and for the Rilke critic Mörchen and Steiner are indispensable, but they do not help the common reader to read Rilke. In all such commentaries it is easy to lose sight of the whole in the bewildering proliferation of cross-referential detail, just as in many studies of the *Elegies* there is little sense of their narrative drive and drama. This introduction, restricting detail and resisting the temptation to annotate at every turn, is simply an attempt to assist the reader of poetry in his or her reading of one of the greatest works in the history of poetry.

Of necessity the guide concentrates exclusively, or almost exclusively, on the meaning of the *Sonnets*, while all the time conscious that the most important aspect, the artistry, is quite another matter. One can explain the first reference to Ovid's Orpheus, but the impact of the startling open image, the tall tree in the ear, an impact depending on sound as well as sense, is lost in any prosaic paraphrase of what it means.[3] Hence one is constantly tempted to have "meaning" in inverted commas, since the reader's response is what it really *means* to the reader, something above and beyond the paraphrase meaning. However, one does inevitably first ask what a poem means and that is what this introduction sets out, prosaically, to answer.

It will be noted that the commentaries on the fifty-five sonnets vary greatly in length. This has nothing to do with the importance or aesthetic merit of the particular sonnet. One is trying to explain the difficulties, not to create them, and some sonnets will seem to need less elucidation. On the other hand a lengthy commentary does not necessarily mean that that sonnet is unusually obscure. It may be, but it may also happen that there is some specific reference, some word or image, which makes it a convenient point to elaborate on some idea fundamental to one's understanding of Rilke.

In a centenary study of Rilke some years ago I adapted Luther's dictum on theologians as a starting point: *sola experientia facit poetam*.[4] Rilke's ideas, it seems to me, are invariably come to by way of analogy with art and the art-experience – something that inevitably leads to the accusation, by some critics, of narcissism, and in a sense Rilke is undoubtedly self-centred. The orphic material, too, is in Rilke essentially a myth on the meaning of music, of poetry. Accordingly, for the sake of those who do not know it already and with apologies to those who do, the guide begins with an account of Rilke's life and work as the context out of which the *Sonnets* come. Some readers will know all this, and much more, and the account is, of course, very summary and slanted towards whatever seems most relevant to the history of the *Sonnets*. But the aim is to make the *Sonnets to Orpheus* accessible to all readers of poetry, whether or not they have had any familiarity with Rilke's work otherwise. In order to cater for the non-specialist, a reader's guide to the *Sonnets to Orpheus* has to be also a reader's guide to Rilke. It is not presupposed even that all readers will be able to read the *Sonnets* without any help from translations. There are several competing translations, but J. B. Leishman's must surely be the one to recommend.[5] Granted the truth of the saying: *traddutore traditore*, Leishman, with his profound knowledge of Rilke, is the translator least likely to betray the poet or mislead the reader.

4

Rilke's Life and Work

Rilke was born on 4 December 1875 in Prague, in the Austro-Hungarian Empire, but he never felt himself to be Austrian or indeed German. It would be hard to say where his spiritual home was – France, Italy, Russia, perhaps, but not forgetting Scandinavia, Spain, Switzerland. While he lived longest in a few places, notably Paris, he did not merely visit most of the major European countries, but absorbed languages and cultures, sometimes composing in other languages, especially French. It would seem that the only major European language and culture he was not at home in was English and on the whole the English-speaking world was alien to him. For the rest he can only be identified as a European. He lived, as a French critic said later, "comme s'il n'avait eu ni patrie, ni famille, ni postérité, ni religion même".[6] In order to understand his present distress, he writes to a friend in September 1915:

> ... müssen Sie sich denken, daß ich nicht "deutsch" empfinde, – in keiner Weise; ob ich gleich dem deutschen Wesen nicht fremd sein kann, da ich in seiner Sprache bis an die Wurzeln ausgebreitet bin, so hat mir doch seine gegenwärtige Anwendung ... nur Befremdung und Kränkung bereitet; und vollends im Österreichischen ... ein Zu-hause zu haben, ist mir rein unausdenkbar und unausfühlbar! Wie soll ich da, ich, dem Rußland, Frankreich, Italien, Spanien, die Wüste und die Bibel das Herz ausgebildet haben, wie soll ich einen Anklang haben zu denen, die hier um mich großsprechen![7]

A few years later the Austrian Government wished to award him the Knight's Cross of the Order of Franz Josef, which he politely declined.

Although, therefore, he was born in one of the most beautiful cities in Europe, Prague does not feature significantly in his work. This has less to do with Prague than with his parental home. After elementary school he went to military academies, although a military training was so inappropriate, indeed grotesque, considering his hypersensitive disposition, compounded by the fact that, whereas his father, whose own military ambitions had been frustrated, wanted an officer son, his mother had wanted a daughter, played make-believe mother-daughter games with René Maria and dressed him as a girl until he was seven years old. Years later one of his old teachers wrote to Rilke asking the now famous poet if he was indeed the same person as the little boy he remembered. The Major-General certainly did not expect such a lengthy letter in reply. (Rilke is one of the great letter writers. His letters number thousands, usually long and elaborate, always courteous not to say courtly, very polished but also very personal to the recipient, a medium of intercourse at once very intimate and at the same time a way of keeping people at a distance, especially his own wife and child.) Rilke leaves the Major-General in no doubt as to the misery of his school-days, comparing the school to Dostoyevsky's *House of the Dead.* The evidence suggests that the school regime was by no means so bad or so hostile to Rilke, but the home constellation could hardly have been less propitious. Any autobiographical hints in the writings suggest that Rilke remembered his father with some affection, perhaps because he had less to do with him after the parents separated, whereas he reacted violently against his mother and by extension against her apparently extravagant and superstitious Catholicism. One of those closest to Rilke in his last years, the

Swiss historian, von Salis, says that Rilke spoke of Christ as he spoke of his mother, with the same shrill note of indignation.[8]

After his schooling a well-to-do uncle was prepared to put him through university, and in a desultory sort of way he studied in Prague and Munich, but in fact his whole and only interest was in writing and in 1894 he published his first collection, which, with its weakly neo-romantic mood-lyricism, like the several following collections in the next four or five years, gives no indication that he was to become one of the greatest European poets. But whatever about the astonishing disparity between the immature and the mature Rilke, consistent is the total dedication to poetry and the life of the poet. Rilke is one of the few poets who lived exclusively by as well as for his poetry, helped by a succession of patrons. There is much facetious comment on Rilke's countless countesses, evidenced by the vast correspondence with countesses, baronesses, princesses, and members generally of the upper classes, who looked after him, sometimes made love to him or put their country manors or town houses at his disposal. This can be exaggerated and in fact his circle of correspondents was wide. Still, he was undoubtedly fastidious and this irritates the more sociologically minded critics, as does his apparent disengagement from the political and social scene. It is true that in some sense he is very unpolitical, partly because of his almost obsessional abhorrence of any kind of interference by anyone in the sphere of anyone else, a recurring motif in his work, for example in *Orpheus. Eurydike. Hermes.* One will find little in his work or correspondence that relates to current affairs, except perhaps in a very indirect or even, with hindsight, ironic way. Thus, for example, one finds him writing on the difficult times they are living in to Countess von Stauffenberg and concluding the letter with the hope that her sons will grow up in more trouble-free times.[9]

One of his literary discoveries during his Munich days was Jens Peter Jacobsen, the Danish novelist, whose psychological realism was the sort of material he badly needed in his own so far too effete neo-romanticism, and who also aroused his interest in Scandinavia, something that bore fruit later, particularly in *Die Aufzeichnungen des Malte Laurids Brigge*, the *Notebooks of Malte Laurids Brigge*, his main prose work. More important still, he got to know Lou Andreas-Salomé, notorious for the intellectual challenge and excitement of her liaisons with Freud, Nietzsche, Wedekind, Rilke among others. She was the daughter of a Russian General and nobleman, growing up with her five brothers in, according to her own memoirs, an idyllically liberal and cultivated household in St Petersburg. There she early began her love life with her pursuit, although she had long lost her faith, of the most popular and handsome Lutheran pastor in St Petersburg. When the pastor wanted to leave wife and family for her, however, she declined, and that was more or less the pattern throughout her life. *She* determined when and at what point affairs started and stopped. She continued her studies in Switzerland, theology, philosophy, comparative religion, art, psychology, later studying and collaborating with Freud and becoming a practising psycho-analyst. She was, said Nietzsche, far and away the cleverest person he had ever met, describing her also as eagle-eyed and lion-hearted. Like so many others, Nietzsche wanted to marry her, but again she declined, though she suggested instead living in a *ménage à trois* with Nietzsche and another philosopher Paul Ree, a scheme that fell through because of the rivalry of the two philosophers. However when Andreas, a Professor of Oriental Languages proposed and she as usual declined, he plunged a knife into his breast – quite seriously and nearly killing himself – and this seems to have so impressed her that she accepted him. On the wedding night she refused to consummate the marriage and she continued to refuse him for the next forty-three years until his death. At the same time she appears to have seen to it that his needs were elsewhere catered for. This, then, was the woman, committed to free love, free living, free thinking, whom Rilke got to know in Munich as an inhibited young man, fourteen years her junior. It was also his introduction to Russia, the country to which he would claim to feel most emotionally akin, though not so much the real pre-revolutionary Russia as the Russia one thinks of as Mother Russia or Holy Russia. He went there first in 1899 with Lou and her accommodating husband, meeting, among others, Tolstoy and the painter Leonid Pasternak with his little boy Boris. As always he learned the language, writing poems in Russian, which, according to Lou, are both ungrammatical and extraordinarily poetic, and immersed himself as much as possible in the spirit of its culture, doubtless with a one-sided pietism, such as informs much of his early work, like the very mannered morality *Tales of the Good God*, or even the more significant book of liturgical poetry, *Das Stundenbuch, The Book of Hours*. In 1900 he went on his second pilgrimage to Russia, this time only with Lou.

Meanwhile, in one of his Italian journeys, he had made the acquaintance of one of the painters from Worpswede, the colony of artists near Bremen, and had made several visits there. There his closest contacts were with Paula Becker, the most gifted painter of the circle, and with the sculptress Clara Westhoff. In 1901 Paula Becker married the painter Modersohn, at that time much better known than she was, and Rilke married Clara Westhoff. They had one child, Ruth. Clara's ambition was to return to Paris, to her model and mentor, Rodin, and this was for Rilke the next decisive step that was to transform him into a great poet, not least under the influence of painting and sculpture generally and of Rodin and Cézanne in particular. It also suited Rilke admirably as they lived apart in Paris. He always maintained that the main concern of marriage partners must be to guard each other's privacy and in his own long separation-marriage he regularly wrote to Clara and to Ruth, explaining how much closer they were, now that they were no longer together. But whatever about this special pleading, his work was greatly strengthened by his intense and penetrating art-studies, which are behind the mature poetry of *New Poems*, but which also have as by-products his own publications on the Worpswede artists and on Rodin. Much of the time that he was writing these, he was living in Italy with short breaks in Denmark and Sweden. In 1905 he moves back to Paris again, this time closer than ever to Rodin, staying with him as his secretary. One of the products of this period is his best-seller prose-poem *The Lay of the Love and Death of Cornet Christopher Rilke*, supposedly known later by every German soldier in the Great War, a narrative of love and death, set in the seventeenth century and centred around a young cornet returning with his regiment from the Turkish assault on Vienna. Like all his works later this was published by the Insel Verlag and it was at this time also that he got to know his publishers, Anton and Katharina Kippenberg, the gifted husband and wife team, who had recently founded the Insel Verlag. As well as being his publishers, the Kippenbergs must be numbered among his patrons, from then on keeping him financially secure – something which proved to be good business, as Rilke became and remained their greatest publishing success.

The other main publication of this period is *Das Stundenbuch, The Book of Hours*, a long three-part poem or sequence of poems, divided into *The Book of Monkish Life, The Book of Pilgrimage* and *The Book of Poverty and Death*. The title derives from the *horae canonicae* of the mediaeval church and the later, mainly French, 15th and 16th century richly decorated breviaries. In Rilke's case it is a kind of cadenced litany, in which the artist-monk explores his relationship to his God – most would say that it is more art-centred than theocentric, but that is not to agree, as many would have it, that it is only about art and the artist, for as always Rilke is widening his reflections into a Weltanschauung, albeit always by way of analogies with art. Rilke himself was critical later of *The Book of Hours*. "I could have gone on composing like that forever", he says dismissively.[10] Still, years later he allowed it some validity. Writing to a reader about the work in 1923 he says:

> Ich fing mit den Dingen an, die die eigentlichen Vertrauten meiner einsamen Kindheit gewesen sind, und es war schon viel, daß ich es, ohne fremde Hilfe, bis zu den Tieren gebracht habe ... Dann aber tat sich mir Rußland auf und schenkte mir die Brüderlichkeit und das Dunkel Gottes, in dem allein Gemeinschaft ist. So nannte ich ihn damals auch, den über mich hereingebrochenen Gott, und lebte lange im Vorraum seines Namens, auf den Knieen ... Jetzt würdest Du mich ihn kaum je nennen hören, es ist eine unbeschreibliche Diskretion zwischen uns, und wo einmal Nähe war und Durchdringung, da spannen sich neue Fernen ... statt des Besitzes erlernt man den Bezug, und es entsteht eine Namenlosigkeit, die wieder bei Gott beginnen muß, um vollkommen und ohne Ausrede zu sein.[11]

Those ideas of non-possession and namelessness are relevant to his orphic myth.

Since the *Book of Hours* is by definition a breviary, it is natural to ask if Rilke believed in God – we may ask the question, but Rilke certainly won't answer it. He is nothing if not evasive, though it is clear enough that, whatever he means by God, it is not a personal transcendental Creator-God. Indeed it would seem to be rather man or at any rate the artist who is the creator. Sometimes it seems as if art is a substitute for religion, or rather Rilke puts it the other way around: religion is the substitute for art. In the *Tuscan Diary* of 1898 he writes:

> Die Religion ist die Kunst der Nichtschaffenden. Im Gebete werden sie produktiv ... Der Nichtkünstler muß eine Religion – im tiefinneren Sinn – besitzen, und sei es auch nur eine, die auf gemeinsamem und historischem Vereinbaren beruht. Atheist sein in seinem Sinne ist Barbar sein.[12]

On the question of faith, too, Rodin is the master and role model. Rilke liked to tell how Rodin was fond of reading the *Imitation of Christ*, but where Thomas a Kempis spoke of God, Rodin would substitute for the word God the word Sculpture, finding that it fitted in exactly. Often enough Rilke expresses belief in a to-be-created future God. When a young poet, Kappus, writes to Rilke, as so many people in trouble did, lamenting his, Kappus', loss of faith Rilke responds:

> Wenn Sie aber erkennen, daß er in Ihrer Kindheit nicht war, daß Christus getäuscht worden ist von seiner Sehnsucht und Muhammed betrogen von seinem Stolze, – und wenn Sie mit Schrecken fühlen, daß er auch jetzt nicht ist, in dieser Stunde, da wir von ihm reden, – was berechtigt Sie dann, ihn, welcher niemals war, wie einen Vergangenen zu vermissen und zu suchen, als ob er verloren wäre? Warum denken Sie nicht, daß er der Kommende ist, der von Ewigkeit her hervorsteht, der Zukünftige, die unendliche Frucht eines Baumes, dessen Blätter wir sind?[13]

Occasionally there are seemingly unequivocal expressions of belief, or rather of unbelief, particularly when it is a case of escaping from that possessiveness, or protectiveness, of which he is obsessively wary. In 1922 he writes to a friend:

> Ein denkendes, ein uns mitwissendes Schicksal
> ... ja, oft wünschte man durch ein solches
> bestärkt und bestätigt zu sein; aber wärs nicht
> zugleich sofort ein uns von außen
> anschauendes, ein uns zuschauendes, mit dem
> wir nicht mehr allein wären? Daß wir einem
> "blinden Schicksal" eingelegt sind, ihm
> innewohnen, ist doch gewissermaßen die
> Bedingung unseres eigenen Blicks, unserer
> schauenden Unschuld. – Erst durch die
> "Blindheit" unseres Schicksals sind wir mit dem
> wunderbar Dumpfen der Welt, das heißt mit
> dem Ganzen, Unübersehlichen und uns
> Übertreffenden recht tief verwandt.[14]

Yet Rilke's language remains throughout a religious one. His creed, however, a questionable one to be sure, is in some sense an affirmation of, a relationship to, a communion with an innocent "whole". So he continues to invoke the gods and God, "in whom alone there is communion", as he said in that letter to Ilse Jahr.

About the only thing one can say with certainty, therefore, about the God of *Das Stundenbuch* is that He is not the God of Christian orthodoxy. Indeed the orthodox images of God are what separates the monk from his neighbour-God:

> Du, Nachbar Gott, wenn ich dich manchesmal
> in langer Nacht mit hartem Klopfen störe, –
> so ists, weil ich dich selten atmen höre
> und weiß: Du bist allein im Saal.
> Und wenn du etwas brauchst, ist keiner da, um
> deinem Tasten einen Trank zu reichen:
> Ich horche immer. Gieb ein kleines Zeichen.
> Ich bin ganz nah.
>
> Nur eine schmale Wand is zwischen uns ...
>
> Aus deinen Bildern ist sie aufgebaut.

> Und deine Bilder stehn vor dir wie Namen.
> Und wenn einmal das Licht in mir entbrennt,
> mit welchem meine Tiefe dich erkennt,
> vergeudet sichs als Glanz auf ihren Rahmen.
>
> Und meine Sinne, welche schnell erlahmen,
> sind ohne Heimat und von dir getrennt.

In his poetry Rilke is a virtuoso of rhyme and rhythm and run-on lines, of assonance and consonance, and this makes him so untranslatable, particularly in the more concentrated forms like the sonnet, as the translators struggle to retain the melody as well as the meaning. The task is easier in the case of longer poems of flowing narrative or reflection and Babette Deutsch's translations[15] from the *Stundenbuch* give the flavour of the original:

> You, neighbour God, if sometimes in the night
> I rouse you with loud knocking, I do so
> only because I seldom hear you breathe;
> I know: you are alone.
> And should you need a drink, no one is there
> to reach it to you, groping in the dark.
> Always I hearken. Give but a small sign.
> I am quite near.
>
> Between us there is but a narrow wall, ...
>
> The wall is builded of your images.
>
> They stand before you hiding you like names,
> And when the light within me blazes high
> that in my inmost soul I know you by,
> the radiance is squandered on their frames.
>
> And then my senses, which too soon grow lame,
> exiled from you, must go their homeless ways.

Sometimes it seems that God is not so much Creator, as being created, work of human hands, like a cathedral, and dependent on the worshipper:

Was wirst du tun, Gott, wenn ich sterbe?
Ich bin dein Krug (wenn ich zerscherbe?)
Ich bin dein Trank (wenn ich verderbe?)
Bin dein Gewand und dein Gewerbe,
mit mir verlierst du deinen Sinn.

Nach mir hast du kein Haus, darin
dich Worte, nah und warm, begrüßen.
Es fällt von deinen müden Füßen
die Samtsandale, die ich bin.

What will you do, God, when I die?
When I, your pitcher, broken, lie?
when I, your drink, go stale or dry?
I am your garb, the trade you ply,
you lose your meaning, losing me.

Homeless without me, you will be
robbed of your welcome, warm and sweet.
I am your sandals: your tired feet
will wander bare for want of me.

To be near God is to be divested of all possessions, an idea that runs throughout Rilke and underlies the "Orpheus. Eurydike. Hermes" poem and the *Elegies* and *Sonnets*. Here, in *The Book of Hours*, Rilke rails, as he so often does, against the idea of possession, thinking not least, one feels, of parental possessiveness:

Du mußt nicht bangen, Gott. Sie sagen: *mein*
zu allen Dingen, die geduldig sind.
Sie sind wie Wind, der an die Zweige streift
und sagt: *mein* Baum.
...

So sagen sie: mein Leben, meine Frau,
mein Hund, mein Kind, und wissen doch genau,
daß alles: Leben, Frau und Hund und Kind
fremde Gebilde sind, daran sie blind
mit ihren ausgestreckten Händen stoßen.

Gewißheit freilich ist das nur den Großen,
die sich nach Augen sehnen. Denn die Andern
wollens nicht hören, daß ihr armes Wandern
mit keinem Dinge rings zusammenhängt,
daß sie, von ihrer Habe fortgedrängt,
nicht anerkannt von ihrem Eigentume,
das Weib so wenig *haben* wie die Blume,
die eines fremden Lebens ist für alle.

Falle nicht, Gott, aus deinem Gleichgewicht.
Auch der dich liebt und der dein Angesicht
erkennt im Dunkel, wenn er wie ein Licht
in deinem Atem schwankt, – besitzt dich nicht.
Und wenn dich einer in der Nacht erfaßt,
so daß du kommen mußt in sein Gebet:
        Du bist der Gast,
        der wieder weiter geht.

Wer kann dich halten, Gott? Denn du bist dein,
von keines Eigentümers Hand gestört,
so wie der noch nicht ausgereifte Wein,
der immer süßer wird, sich selbst gehört.

Do not be troubled, God, though they say "mine"
of all things that permit it patiently.
They are like wind that lightly strokes the boughs
and says: MY tree.

And so they say: my life, my wife, my child,
my dog, well knowing all that they have styled
their own: life, wife, child, dog, remain
shapes alien and unknown,
that blindly groping they must stumble on.
This truth, be sure, only the great discern,
who long for eyes. The others WILL not learn
that in the beggary of their wandering
they cannot claim a bond with any thing,
but, driven from possessions they have prized,
not by their own belongings recognized,
they can OWN wives no more than they own flowers,
whose life is alien and apart from ours.

God, do not lose your equilibrium.
Even he who loves you and who knows your face
in darkness, when he trembles like a light
you breathe upon, – he cannot own you quite.
And if at night one holds you closely pressed,
locked in his prayer so you cannot stray,
> you are the guest
> who comes, but not to stay.

God, who can hold you? To yourself alone
belonging, by no owner's hand disturbed,
you are like unripened wine that unperturbed
grows ever sweeter and is all its own.

Brecht spoke derisively of Rilke's homosexual affair with God in *Das Stundenbuch* and the mockery is not so inappropriate, for there is something, if not "schwul", "queer", the term Brecht uses, then "schwül" in the sense of a sultry sensuousness, part indeed of its erotic appeal:

Mach Einen herrlich, Herr, mach Einen groß,
bau seinem Leben einen schönen Schooß,
und seine Scham errichte wie ein Tor
in einem blonden Wald von jungen Haaren,
und ziehe durch das Glied des Unsagbaren
den Reisigen, den weißen Heeresscharen,
den tausend Samen, die sich sammeln, vor.

Und eine Nacht gieb, daß der Mensch empfinge
was keines Menschen Tiefen noch betrat;
gieb eine Nacht: da blühen alle Dinge,
und mach sie duftender als die Syringe
und wiegender denn deines Windes Schwinge
und jubelnder als Josaphat.

In the translation by J. B. Leishman:[16]

> Make someone glorious, Lord, make someone great,
> build a fine womb for him, and, like a gate
> within a flaxen forest of young hair,
> erect its entrance, and, yourself advancing
> through the unmentioned member, lead those prancing
> cavalry in, those hosts all whitely glancing,
> those myriad seeds that are assembled there.
>
> And grant a night that to mankind here brings
> more than all human depths have quivered at;
> make it a night all full of flowering things,
> and sweeter than syringa's perfumings,
> and more sleep-rocking than your wind's own wings,
> and more rejoicing than Jehosaphat.

The mere religiosity of the work would, of course, be enough to offend Brecht and many other readers, but their objection is more specific. Probably the most ill-famed line in all of Rilke is the line from *Das Stundenbuch*:

> For poverty is a great radiance from within
>
> Denn Armut is ein großer Glanz aus Innen ...

a line that introduces his invocation of God in a litany of poverty images:

> Du bist der Arme, du der Mittellose,
> du bist der Stein, der keine Stätte hat,
> du bist der fortgeworfene Leprose,
> der mit der Klapper umgeht vor der Stadt.
>
> Denn dein ist nichts, so wenig wie des Windes,
> und deine Blöße kaum bedeckt der Ruhm;
> das Alltagskleidchen eines Waisenkindes
> ist herrlicher und wie ein Eigentum.
>
> Und was sind Vögel gegen dich, die frieren,
> was ist ein Hund, der tagelang nicht fraß,
> und was ist gegen dich das Sichverlieren,
> das stille lange Traurigsein von Tieren,
> die man als Eingefangene vergaß?

In the translation by A. L. Peck:[17]

> You are the poor one, of all wealth denuded,
> you are the stone for which no place is found,
> you are the leper, outcast and excluded,
> rattle in hand, outside the city's bound.
>
> Nothing you own, bare as the winds that wander;
> and your renown scarce hides your nakedness;
> the weekday clothes an orphan wears are grander,
> more like a property he can possess.
>
> ...
>
> The birds that shiver can't with you compare,
> the dog that's had no food the livelong day,
> the loss of self, uncertainty's despair
> of beasts' long sad existence, dumb and drear,
> in some forgotten outhouse locked away.

The exaltation of poverty disturbs many critics, but without going into the problem of the social and political aspect – and if one wants to attack Rilke on those grounds, there is much more damaging evidence elsewhere – suffice it to say here that the poverty of which he speaks in *The Book of Hours* relates to that idea of non-possession and to the ideal of total openness as represented by St. Francis, the patron saint of *The Book of Hours*, which terminates with the graphic description, highly significant in any consideration of Rilke's beliefs, of the death of St. Francis:

> Und als er starb, so leicht wie ohne Namen,
> da war er ausgeteilt: sein Samen rann
> in Bächen, in den Bäumen sang sein Samen
> und sah ihn ruhig aus den Blumen an.
> Er lag und sang. Und als die Schwestern kamen,
> da weinten sie um ihren lieben Mann.
>
> And when he died, so lightly, like with no name,
> He was distributed; his seed ran
> into the rivers, from the trees his seed sang
> and looked upon him calmly from the flowers.

He lay and sang. And there the sisters came
Their own beloved husband to bewail.

Perhaps in the end it is best to think of *The Book of Hours* in the way that Eudo Mason suggests.[18] The real theme of the *Book of Hours*, says Mason is:

> Rilke's own inner life, the vibrations and oscillations of a hovering, dithyrambic soul, the sinking and soaring of his aspirations and, above all, his sense ... of his vocation, his creative powers and also his perils as a poet. Those are the things he cannot – at least at this stage – express without using the supreme figure of speech – *God*. (Later, indeed, he was to use other images and symbols for the same purpose, particularly the angel of the *Elegies* and the Orpheus of the *Sonnets*.)

Much that could be said about the God of *The Book of Hours*, therefore, could also be said of Rilke's Orpheus. Sometimes there are echoes in the *Sonnets* from the earlier work. "Du kommst und gehst" in the first part of *The Book of Hours* is echoed in the Orpheus-defining fifth sonnet: "Er kommt und geht".

The Book of Hours was published in 1905, *Cornet* in 1906. In the following four years four major works appeared: *New Poems* in 1907, *New Poems Part Two* in 1908, *Requiem* in 1909 and *The Notebooks of Malte Laurids Brigge* in 1910. The new poems are mostly of the kind usually referred to as Rilkes "Dinggedichte" or thing-poems, characterized by a new respect for and concentration on things in their own right, rather than as objects of the poet's subjective moods and emotions, and the aim is to recreate their thingness, their quiddity, a reaction against what Rilke himself called his earlier cheap approximation, "billiges à peu près", in favour of precision. They are the result of years of studying the visual arts and his observation of Rodin's works and working habits. Two of the best-known poems may serve as examples, "The Panther" and "Archaic Torso of Apollo".

The story goes that when Rilke complained to Rodin about the difficulties of artistic creation, Rodin advised him to look at things, to go, for example, to the zoo and look at the animals, the result being the poem on the panther, depicting the caged animal, not described from the outside, but seeing its situation from within, as the bars pass him in endless circular procession. On the one hand the subject matter is simple, and the poem is a favourite anthology piece, but it is also puzzling, particularly in the last stanza, when, from time to time, the tense, cramped movement of the panther is interrupted, as an image from the outer world enters the eye of the animal and is as quickly extinguished. Some critics understand this very positively, for example seeing the image that enters the heart as that which nourishes the inner life, being extinguished in the sense that it is absorbed by the animal, or, by metaphorical extension, by man. For others the panther of the poem, robbed of its freedom and benumbed, is a subject without an object, cut off from the world, and the panther becomes a metaphor for that man who is unable to inwardise the outer world and is bereft of reality. In particular the panther becomes for some the metaphor of the poet imprisoned in the isolation of his narcissism and unable to take in the world outside – though one may well argue that this is precisely what the poet here is doing. And not only can the closing lines be seen positively or negatively, they can, as it were, be read negatively positively. One of the marxist critics understands it positively as an inner transformation, an absorption of the outer world into that inner-world-space, "Weltinnenraum", of which Rilke so often speaks, a foretaste of what is to come in the *Elegies* and *Sonnets* – only it is a positive meaning which the critic himself heartily dislikes and excoriates as an effete and ineffectual bourgeois aestheticism, sympathising with the rather more fantastic interpretation of Bert Brecht – whether serious or merely sardonic – who maintains that the panther, the beautiful aristocratic beast, now tamed and caged, is a metaphor for the French aristocracy and their present plight, now all too sentimentally seen and sung by a bourgeois poet.[19] There is a choice of metaphorical meanings, though one also asks oneself if one should be looking for metaphorical meaning. For one of the effects of these thing-poems, so immediately reminiscent of the visual and plastic arts, is that one does inevitably ask what they mean, but at the same time wonder if the question is any more, or in any different way, meaningful than if we asked it of one of Rodin's bronzes. In any case what communicates itself to most readers is the perfection of form, the taut construction that is the objective correlative of the pent-up energy and constriction that is its subject-matter:

DER PANTHER
Im Jardin des Plantes, Paris

Sein Blick ist vom Vorübergehn der Stäbe
so müd geworden, daß er nichts mehr hält.
Ihm ist, als ob es tausend Stäbe gäbe
Und hinter tausend Stäben keine Welt.

Der weiche Gang geschmeidig starker Schritte,
der sich im allerkleinsten Kreise dreht,
ist wie ein Tanz von Kraft um eine Mitte,
in der betäubt ein großer Wille steht.

Nur manchmal schiebt der Vorhang der Pupille
sich lautlos auf –. Dann geht ein Bild hinein,
geht durch der Glieder angespannte Stille –
und hört im Herzen auf zu sein.

In Walter Arndt's translation:[20]

His gaze has been so worn by the procession
Of bars that it no longer makes a bond.
Around, a thousand bars seem to be flashing,
And in their flashing show no world beyond.

> The lissom steps which round out and re-enter
> That tightest circuit of their turning drill
> Are like a dance of strength about a center
> Wherein there stands benumbed a mighty will.
> Only from time to time the pupil's shutter
> Will draw apart: an image enters then,
> To travel through the tautened body's utter
> Stillness – and in the heart to end.

Much of course depends on the phonological effect, for example here the succession of long vowels and diphthongs. Not a great deal of this comes across in translation. Walter Arndt publishes together with his translation his strictures on several other translations, showing point by point where they go wrong. But one can also say that his own translation does not with its flashing bars convey the sense of weary, hypnotic monotony of the original.

"Archaic Torso of Apollo" has a more recherché theme, though it is perhaps less open to conflicting interpretations. It was inspired by a 5th century B.C. torso in the Louvre. The way that Rilke looked at such things is suggested, for example, in a letter (of ten printed pages) in 1903 to Lou:

> Darin, glaube ich, liegt der unvergleichliche Wert dieser wiedergefundenen Dinge, daß man sie so ganz wie Unbekannte betrachten kann; man kennt ihre Absicht nicht und es hängt sich (für den Unwissenschaftlichen wenigstens) nichts Stoffliches an sie an, keine nebensächliche Stimme unterbricht die Stille ihres gesammelten Daseins ... kein mißverstandener Ruhm färbt ihre Formen, die rein sind, keine Geschichte überschattet ihre entkleidete Klarheit –: sie sind. Und das ist alles. So denke ich mir die antikische Kunst.[21]

Another relevant letter is one to his wife in 1902, in which he says that for Rodin an arm or leg, a thigh or torso is something complete and closed within itself, because he no longer sees it as part of something else – to see it in that fragmentary way would seem to him too material, too novelistic so to speak, "zu stofflich, zu novellistisch sozusagen".[22]

This primacy of form, that mystery to most, as Goethe calls it, over "stoffliches Interesse" or material interest is part of the idea of the Rilke poem. The torso is seen as still infused with and informed by the vision in the head's eyesight. It is as if the power of sight were screwed back into the torso, turned down like the wick of a candelabrum. The torso is still gazing at us, still smiling at its procreative centre. The context of this odd reference to the smile and its location may be Rilke's resentment about and rebellion against what he felt from his Catholic upbringing to be the Christian distortion of sexuality. This is particularly documented in what he calls the "letter of a young workman", *Brief eines jungen Arbeiters* of 1922, in which he dilates on the repressions of Christianity – and of course the poem here is on a pagan artefact and a pagan God. However, that is only a detail, and the main thrust of the poem is the torso as, paradoxically, an image of integrity, radiant and complete, and a reproach to man in his imperfection and fragmentariness. Hence the sudden and startling final phrase: you must change your life. The idea of the ethical effect of ancient art goes back to Winckelmann and to those that followed him, particularly to Goethe, who speaks of himself in Rome as having been changed "to the innermost marrow", as indeed, anyone must be "who seriously looks around himself here and has eyes to see".[23] And one can, of course, relate the closing phrase to the inscription: Know Thyself, in the entrance hall of Apollo's shrine in Delphi.

Archaïscher Torso Apollos

Wir kannten nicht sein unerhörtes Haupt,
darin die Augenäpfel reiften. Aber
sein Torso glüht noch wie ein Kandelaber,
in dem sein Schauen, nur zurückgeschraubt,

sich hält und glänzt. Sonst könnte nicht der Bug
der Brust dich blenden, und im leisen Drehen
der Lenden könnte nicht ein Lächeln gehen
zu jener Mitte, die die Zeugung trug.

Sonst stünde dieser Stein entstellt und kurz
unter der Schultern durchsichtigem Sturz
und flimmerte nicht so wie Raubtierfelle;

und bräche nicht aus allen seinen Rändern
aus wie ein Stern: denn da ist keine Stelle,
die dich nicht sieht. Du mußt dein Leben ändern.

In Stephen Mitchell's translation:[24]

> We cannot know his legendary head
> with eyes like ripening fruit. And yet his torso
> is still suffused with brilliance from inside,
> like a lamp, in which his gaze, now turned to low,
>
> gleams in all its power. Otherwise
> the curved breast could not dazzle you so, nor could
> a smile run through the placid hips and thighs
> to that dark center where procreation flared.
>
> Otherwise this stone would seem defaced
> beneath the translucent cascade of the shoulders
> and would not glisten like a wild beast's fur:
>
> would not, from all the borders of itself,
> burst like a star: for here there is no place
> that does not see you. You must change your life.

To suggest the meaning of the poem does not give much idea of its power as a tightly constructed sonnet, held together, not only by alliteration and assonance, end-rhyme and internal rhyme, but – appropriately for the God of Light – by a network of optical verbs and nouns: Augenäpfel, Kandelaber, Stern, glühen, schauen, glänzen, blenden, flimmern, sehen. Much of this has to get lost in translation, as has the force of the subjunctives in the centre of the poem, reflecting the strangeness of the phenomenon it describes.

Among the *New Poems* was "Orpheus. Eurydike. Hermes", discussed separately below. It was at the time of these poems that Rilke first met Princess Marie von Thurn und Taxis-Hohenlohe, at whose castle in Duino, near Trieste, Rilke began his most famous work, the *Duino Elegies*. Lou Andreas-Salomé and Princess Marie von Thurn und Taxis were the two most important friends in his life and it was to both of them that he turned with all his troubles, sure of sympathy and support from both, though in different ways. Whereas Lou counselled more professionally, Princess Marie, as well as mothering him – she was twenty years older – scolded him for his disastrous entanglements whenever he left his isolation, though she also usually reminded him and herself that if he were not so crazy he would not be such a genius, so for the sake of his poetry he had better not reform. With her influence, she was of great practical help, but she was also one of Rilke's most understanding readers. She was a gifted musician and linguist, who translated philosophical works into French and Rilke into Italian. Also she was blessed with common sense and a sense of humour. She was a member of the London Society for Psychical Research, and Rilke, like Yeats, became interested in spiritualism, though to a much lesser degree and influenced by Princess Marie's relaxed attitude.

The spirit world features more significantly in Rilke's next major publication, related to the Orpheus/Eurydike theme. *Requiem* consists of two long requiem poems, one on a young poet, Wolf Graf von Kalckreuth, whom Rilke had not known personally, but of whose suicide he had heard, leading Rilke to reflect on the salvation the young poet might have found in his art. Had he waited he might have had the saving experience of the artist, whose fate enters his work and becomes something, someone else, albeit vaguely familar, like the portrait of some distant ancestor. That requiem ends with one of the most quoted lines in Rilke:

Who talks of victory? To endure is all.

Wer spricht von Siegen? Überstehn ist alles.

But the other, longer requiem is more relevant here. This is a requiem for Paula Modersohn-Becker, the most gifted painter of the Worpswede group. Rilke had probably been in love with her and some would see his marriage to her friend Clara Westhoff as a reaction after her engagement to Otto Modersohn, the director of the artists' colony. Soon after her marriage Paula took leave from Worpswede and went to Paris to paint, but was reminded by letters from her husband and her parents of her wifely duties. She duly came home, became pregnant, gave birth to a child in 1907 and died a week or two later. This gives rise to Rilke's reflections in the requiem on the ancient enmity, for the artist, between life and work, a poem, therefore, partly on the Yeats theme:

A man must choose
perfection of the life or of the work

– a choice that Rilke sees as still more painful in the case of a woman. As a longer, more narrative type poem it is more translatable. Its opening lines address the ghost of Paula, who is haunting him:

> Ich habe Tote, und ich ließ sie hin
> und war erstaunt, sie so getrost zu sehn,
> so rasch zuhaus im Totsein, so gerecht,
> so anders als ihr Ruf. Nur du, du kehrst
> zurück; du streifst mich, du gehst um, du willst
> an etwas stoßen, daß es klingt von dir
> und dich verrät. O nimm mir nicht, was ich
> langsam erlern. Ich habe recht; du irrst
> wenn du gerührt zu irgend einem Ding
> ein Heimweh hast. Wir wandeln dieses um;
> es ist nicht hier, wir spiegeln es herein
> aus unserm Sein, sobald wir es erkennen.
> Ich glaubte dich viel weiter. Mich verwirrts,
> daß *du* gerade irrst und kommst, die mehr
> verwandelt hat als irgend eine Frau.

In Stephen Mitchell's translation:

> I have my dead, and I have let them go,
> and was amazed to see them so contented,
> so soon at home in being dead, so cheerful,
> so unlike their reputation. Only you
> return; brush past me, loiter, try to knock
> against something, so that the sound reveals
> your presence. Oh don't take from me what I
> am slowly learning. I'm sure you have gone astray
> if you are moved to homesickness for anything
> in this dimension. We transform these Things;
> they aren't real, they are only the reflections
> upon the polished surface of our being.
> I thought you were much farther on. It troubles me
> that you should stray back, you, who have achieved
> more transformation than any other woman.

Many themes are touched on in the long recall that follows, until finally he recalls her death and the neglected lamentation, though it may be less lamentation, "Klage", that is needed than accusation, "Anklage":

    ... Doch jetzt klag ich an:
den Einen nicht, der dich aus dir zurückzog,
(ich find ihn nicht heraus, er ist wie alle)
doch alle klag ich in ihm an: den Mann.

    ... Denn dieses Leiden dauert schon zu lang,
und keiner kanns; es ist zu schwer für uns,
das wirre Leiden von der falschen Liebe,
die, bauend auf Verjährung wie Gewohnheit,
ein Recht sich nennt und wuchert aus dem Unrecht.
Wo ist ein Mann, der Recht hat auf Besitz?
Wer kann besitzen, was sich selbst nicht hält,
was sich von Zeit zu Zeit nur selig auffängt
und wieder hinwirft wie ein Kind den Ball.
Sowenig wie der Feldherr eine Nike
festhalten kann am Vorderbug des Schiffes,
wenn das geheime Leichtsein ihrer Gottheit
sie plötzlich weghebt in den hellen Meerwind:
so wenig kann einer von uns die Frau
anrufen, die uns nicht mehr sieht und die
auf einem schmalen Streifen ihres Daseins
wie durch ein Wunder fortgeht, ohne Unfall:
er hätte denn Beruf und Lust zur Schuld.
 Denn das ist Schuld, wenn irgendeines Schuld ist:
die Freiheit eines Lieben nicht vermehren
um alle Freiheit, die man in sich aufbringt.
Wir haben, wo wir lieben, ja nur dies:
einander lassen; denn daß wir uns halten,
das fällt uns leicht und ist nicht erst zu lernen.
...

But now I must accuse:
not the man who withdrew you from yourself
(I cannot find him; he looks like everyone),
but in this one man, I accuse: all men.

...

For this suffering has lasted far too long;
none of us can bear it; it is too heavy –
this tangled suffering of spurious love
which, building on convention like a habit,
calls itself just, and fattens on injustice.
Show me a man with a right to his possession.

> Who can possess what cannot hold its own self,
> but only, now and then, will blissfully
> catch itself, then quickly throw itself
> away, like a child playing with a ball.
> As little as a captain can hold the carved
> Nike facing outward from his ship's prow
> when the lightness of her godhead suddenly
> lifts her up, into the bright sea-wind:
> so little can one of us call back the woman
> who, now no longer seeing us, walks on
> along the narrow strip of her existence
> as though by miracle, in perfect safety –
> unless, that is, he wishes to do wrong.
> For this is wrong, if anything is wrong:
> not to enlarge the freedom of a love
> with all the inner freedom one can summon.
> We need, in love, to practice only this:
> letting each other go. For holding on
> comes easily; we do not need to learn it.

In the final passage the Yeats theme is summed up in the lines:

> Denn irgendwo ist eine alte Feindschaft
> zwischen dem Leben und der großen Arbeit.

> For somewhere there is an ancient enmity
> between our daily life and the great work.

Overall, with the rejection of possessiveness and holding on, there is an obvious reversal of the Eurydice story, Orpheus returning Eurydice to the underworld.

Requiem was published in 1909 and in the following year came Rilke's main prose work: *The Notebooks of Malte Laurids Brigge*. In a qualified sense Malte is an *alter ego* figure for Rilke, though Rilke always insisted that he should not be identified with Malte, who is kept at an ironic distance. Malte is the twenty-eight year old scion of an ancient Danish family, living in Paris, and the notebooks are the observations, reflections, self-analyses of a hyper-sensitive, not to say neurotic young poet. Much of it is concerned with the minutiae of city life, particularly in its darker aspects, with the world of beggars, asylums, hospitals. The opening sentence reads in Stephen Spender's translation:

> People come here then to live? I should rather have thought that they come here to die.

The translation does not convey the sense of anonymity in the passive form of the original:

> So, also hierher kommen die Leute, um zu leben,
> ich würde eher meinen, es stürbe sich hier.

In his neurotic fashion Malte makes the most exact and disturbingly detailed observation of objects and records people's gestures, habits, tics, sometimes indeed their neuroses. There is the story, for example, of Nikolaj Kusmitsch, the young Russian, who lives in the room next to Malte, reciting Pushkin to himself all day and never leaving his bed. Eventually Malte learns why the man never gets up. It appears that he hit one day on the idea of calculating the number of years, months, days, minutes, seconds he could expect to have left, and was impressed by the resulting figures. He became obsessed with the aim of husbanding this wealth and did his best to save time, getting up ever earlier, running to work and the like, but according to his week-end calculations all in vain. Soon he becomes so conscious of the passage of time, it is like a breeze blowing past him, so that he seems to be sitting perpetually in a draught. He gets up and walks around, but then remembers how the earth rotates, which further unsettles him, and when he recalls from his schooldays something about the angle of the earth's axis, he loses his footing altogether. Since then he has stayed in bed. So Nikolaj Kusmitsch is a grotesque figure of existential angst, representative of the Age of Anxiety. The Paris scenes are interspersed with nostalgic memories of his Danish home, transformations of Rilke's own memories of Prague and elsewhere. The notebooks end with the retelling and reversal of the story of the Prodigal Son, for in the retelling it becomes the legend of one who is trying to escape from the love that seeks to possess him.

Shortly after the publication of *Malte*, in the winter of 1911–12 Rilke spent his first months in Princess Marie's castle at Duino, near Trieste. How he came to begin writing the *Elegies* is dramatically described by Princess Marie in her memoirs:[25]

> Rilke erzählte mir später, wie diese Elegie enstanden war. Er ahnte nichts von dem, was sich in ihm vorbereitete ... er begann zu glauben, daß auch dieser Winter ohne Ergebnis bleiben würde.
>
> Da erhielt er eines Tages einen lästigen geschäftlichen Brief. Er wollte ihn rasch erledigen und mußte sich mit Ziffern und anderen trockenen Dingen abgeben. Draußen blies eine heftige Bora, aber die Sonne schien, das Meer leuchtete blau, wie mit Silber übersponnen. Rilke stieg zu den Bastionen hinunter, die, vom Meer aus nach Osten und Westen gelegen, durch einen schmalen Weg am Fuße des Schlosses verbunden waren. Die Felsen fallen dort steil, wohl an 200 Fuß tief, ins Meer hinab. Rilke ging ganz in Gedanken versunken auf und ab, da die Antwort auf den Brief ihn sehr beschäftigte. Da, auf einmal, mitten in seinem Grübeln, blieb er stehen, plötzlich, denn es war ihm, als ob im Brausen des Sturmes eine Stimme ihm zugerufen hätte:
>
> "Wer, wenn ich schriee, hörte mich denn aus der Engel Ordnungen?"
> Lauschend blieb er stehen. "Was ist das?" flüsterte er halblaut ... "was ist es, was kommt?"
> Er nahm sein Notizbuch, das er stets mit sich führte, und schrieb diese Worte nieder und gleich dazu noch einige Verse, die sich ohne sein Dazutun formten.

> Wer kam? Er wußte es jetzt: der Gott ...
> Sehr ruhig stieg er wieder in sein Zimmer hinauf, legte sein Notizbuch beiseite und erledigte den Geschäftsbrief.
> Am Abend aber war die ganze Elegie niedergeschrieben. Kurz darauf sollte die zweite, die Engel-Elegie, folgen.

It is a scene that captured the imagination of many, not least his fellow-poets. So, for example, the young English poet, Sidney Keyes, wrote – with an odd assessment of "learning" – in one of his longer poems:[26]

> were I to speak out clear
> In that high house, a voice of light might answer.
> Once a man cried and the great Orders heard him:
> Pacing upon a windy wall at night
> A pale unlearned poet out of Europe's
> Erratic heart cried and was filled with speech ...

This was only the beginning of the *Elegies*, and for the next ten years Rilke struggled to continue and complete what he was convinced must be his magnum opus. His peripatetic life became more restless than ever and he was tormented by feelings of aridity, though in fact those years were by no means unproductive. Most accounts of Rilke's development point to a poem of 1914 called "Wendung", change or new direction, with the lines:

> Werk des Gesichts ist getan,
> tue nun Herz-Werk

– work of vision is done, now do heart-work – reminding one of Cézanne's "the eye is not enough" and in which Rilke seems to be exhorting himself to go forward to a stage beyond the thing-poems towards the more reflective poems of his later period.

Two short poems may serve as examples of the post-Duino poetry. "Ausgesetzt auf den Bergen des

Herzens," "Exposed on the hills of the heart" is one of the most persistent themes, underlying also the *Elegies* and *Sonnets*, the theme of the consciousness that separates man from the rest of creation. The poem most immediately recalls Hopkins' "O the mind, mind has mountains". Rilke's poem is built around the contrast between man's self-conscious uncertainty and the sure-footed security of other creatures.

> Ausgesetzt auf den Bergen des Herzens. Siehe, wie klein dort,
> siehe: die letzte Ortschaft der Worte, und höher,
> aber wie klein auch, noch ein letztes
> Gehöft von Gefühl. Erkennst du's?
> Ausgesetzt auf den Bergen des Herzens. Steingrund
> unter den Händen. Hier blüht wohl
> einiges auf; aus stummem Absturz
> blüht ein unwissendes Kraut singend hervor.
> Aber der Wissende? Ach, der zu wissen begann
> und schweigt nun, ausgesetzt auf den Bergen des Herzens.
> Da geht wohl, heilen Bewußtseins,
> manches umher, manches gesicherte Bergtier,
> wechselt und weilt. Und der große geborgene Vogel
> kreist um der Gipfel reine Verweigerung. – Aber
> ungeborgen, hier auf den Bergen des Herzens ...

In J. B. Leishman's translation:[27]

> Exposed on the heart's mountains. Look, how small there!
> look, the last hamlet of words, and, higher,
> farmstead of feeling: d'you see it?
> Exposed on the heart's mountains. Virgin rock
> under the hands. Though even here
> something blooms: from the dumb precipice
> an unknowing plant blooms singing into the air.
> But what of the knower? Ah, he began to know
> and holds his peace, exposed on the heart's mountains.
> While, with undivided mind,
> many, maybe, many well-assured mountain beasts,
> pass there and pause. And the mighty sheltered bird
> circles the summits' pure refusal.– But, oh,
> no longer sheltered, here on the heart's mountains ...

The second poem, "Tränen, Tränen, die aus mir brechen", on the theme of death, serves to remind one of the limitations of paraphrasing explication. Reading the Rilke literature, one is struck by the fact that many critics, perhaps particularly those writing in English, like Eudo Mason or Michael Hamburger, take issue with Rilke's ideas, while acknowledging his supremacy as a poet. This touches on the basic problem, such as is addressed in, for example, Michael Hamburger's *The Truth of Poetry*. The appropriateness of judging poetry in terms of ideas is questionable and subject to qualification. In one of his essays[28] T. S. Eliot says:

> I doubt whether belief proper enters into the activity of a great poet, *qua* poet ... Dante, *qua* poet, did not believe or disbelieve the Thomist theology or theory of the soul: he merely made use of it, or a fusion took place between his initial emotional impulses and a theory, for the purpose of making poetry.

But of course poets do, Rilke certainly did, want to widen their context into a whole Weltanschauung. Yet several critics dismiss his ideas. A representative of that scepticism among the German critics is Hans Egon Holthusen. Holthusen writes:

> Once abstracted from the concrete liveliness of their metaphorical language, from their aesthetic context, and regarded as philosophical doctrine, Rilke's "ideas" are wrong. ... The idea of "my own death" is wrong because death ... must always remain wholly other than ourselves, a conquest through that which is alien to us, an invasion of human reality by a reality that is more than human. The idea of love that abdicates from possession is wrong: so is the idea ... of immanence without transcendence ... the dissolving of God into inwardness. All these ideas are as wrong as the prophetic theses of Nietzsche – the doctrine of the Eternal Recurrence, of the Superman – or the "satanism" of Baudelaire.[29]

This does not make Holthusen any the less appreciative of Rilke as a poet, and the poem which he then goes on to quote enthusiastically, as an example of a Rilke who had gone beyond philosophy and even myth-making into the more mysterious sphere of the inexplicable and in a sense unsayable is the poem given here: "Tränen, Tränen, die aus mir brechen", "Tears, tears, which break forth from me":

> Tränen, Tränen, die aus mir brechen.
> Mein Tod, Mohr, Träger
> meines Herzens, halte mich schräger,
> daß sie abfließen. Ich will sprechen.
>
> Schwarzer, riesiger Herzhalter,
> Wenn ich auch spräche,
> glaubst du denn, daß das Schweigen bräche?
>
> Wiege mich, Alter.

In J. P. Stern's version, in his translation of the Holthusen study:

> Tears, oh tears which break forth from me.
> My death, oh Moor, bearer of my heart,
> hold me steeper, deeper,
> let them run down. I want to speak.
>
> Giant black heart-holder
> And if I spoke
> do you think, then, the silence would break?
> Rock me, old friend.

Holthusen says of this poem:

> It is as if, with this small poem of indescribable sweetness and beauty, the *appassionato* of the *Elegies* were to be surpassed by a brief *dolce e cantabile*: a blackamoor lullaby, a sweet *cantilena* ... The hymnic fervour of the *Tenth Elegy* ... has now been left behind ... The poet knows that it is

inexpressible, this strange, melancholy being-in-the-world which is so heavy with tears, and his very abdication from expressing it all gives us lyrical verse the like of which does not exist in modern German poetry: a *bel canto* that hides the mystery within itself. Here if anywhere the call *ecce poeta* is valid, in the face of all theological criticism.

Holthusen eulogises the poem in altogether musical terms, *dolce e cantabile*, a *cantilena*, a *bel canto*, a salutary reminder that one should respond to a poem as one would respond to music or other art-forms. And yet, of course, one does ask what it means, the last line for example. The old "friend" of the translation is a gratuitous addition, though it may well be true to the spirit of the poem, and the translation "rock me" for "wiege mich" is not necessarily the whole truth of the original. "Wiege" is the imperative of the regular verb "wiegen", to rock, but it is also the imperative of the irregular verb "wiegen", to weigh, which suggests a different interpretation. Rilke was interested in Egyptian mythology, had been in Egypt some years before and was certainly familiar with the motif of the Egyptian God of the Dead, Anubis, who is depicted as weighing the heart of man after death. Probably both meanings are intended.

In the ten years between 1912 and 1922 Rilke moves from place to place, making many attempts to continue with the *Elegies*, moving in 1919 to Switzerland in search of a suitable refuge and finally settling in the Château de Muzot in the canton of Wallis. In 1922 comes the extraordinary breakthrough when, within a matter of days at the beginning of February he completes the *Ten Elegies* and, as a totally unexpected by-product, the 55 *Sonnets to Orpheus*. This again is dramatically described in his own euphoric letters to the Princess, to Lou and to Anton Kippenberg. To his publisher he writes:[30]

Mein lieber Freund,

spät, und ob ich gleich kaum mehr die Feder halten kann, nach einigen Tagen ungeheuern Gehorsams im Geiste –, es muß ... *Ihnen* muß es noch heute, jetzt noch, eh ich zu schlafen versuche, gesagt sein:
ich bin überm Berg!
Endlich! Die Elegien sind da ...

...

So.
Lieber Freund, jetzt erst werde ich atmen und, gefaßt, an Handliches gehen. Denn dieses war überlebensgroß –, ich habe gestöhnt in diesen Tagen und Nächten, wie damals in Duino –, aber, selbst nach jenem Ringen dort –, ich habe nicht gewußt, daß ein solcher Sturm aus Geist und Herz über einen kommen kann! Daß mans übersteht! daß mans übersteht.
Genug, es ist da.
Ich bin hinausgegangen, in den kalten Mondschein und habe das kleine Muzot gestreichelt wie ein großes Tier –, die alten Mauern, die mirs gewährt haben.

This has become one of the most famous examples of poetic inspiration and is recalled, for example, by W. H. Auden in his poem "In Time of War":

When all the apparatus of report
Confirms the triumph of our enemies;
Our bastion pierced, our army in retreat,
Violence successful like a new disease,

And Wrong a charmer everywhere invited;
When we regret that we were ever born:
Let us remember all who seemed deserted.
Tonight in China let me think of one,

Who through ten years of silence worked and waited,
Until in Muzot all his powers spoke,
And everything was given once for all:

And with the gratitude of the Completed
He went out in the winter night to stroke
That little tower like a great animal.

In the few years left to him after the *Elegies* and *Sonnets* Rilke continued to feel that he had accomplished his life's work, but he also wrote some of his finest German poems as well as a large body of poems in French. But his health deteriorated rapidly and after a long and painful illness, documented in letters as he tries to come to terms with the realities of sickness and death, he died of leukemia at the end of 1926 and was buried, as he requested, in the graveyard of the little church of Raron near Muzot, with the lines inscribed on his gravestone as he had directed in his testament:

Rose, o pure contradiction, delight,
In being nobody's sleep under so many
lids.

Rose, oh reiner Widerspruch, Lust,
Niemandes Schlaf zu sein unter soviel
Lidern.

This is the best-known epitaph in modern German literature, as the epitaph of Yeats is the most famous in the English context. The last entry in his diary, probably around mid-December 1926, is the draft of a final poem, still unfinished and unpolished, as Rilke struggles to retain his faith in the face of a totally new and alien situation. It is intensely moving and particularly important if one were inclined to dismiss his variations on the death motif as an all too romantic mythology or even posturing. Here in this poem with its imagery of isolation and naked pain, without past or future and with only the presence of death, Rilke finally invokes as his last subject what he calls "heilloser Schmerz", a terrible phrase that suggests not merely incurable pain, but pain that seems to have no meaning, no teleology, no redemption, and that yet must be, and is, included in his acceptance:

> Komm du, du letzter, den ich anerkenne,
> heilloser Schmerz im leiblichem Geweb:
> wie ich im Geiste brannte, sieh, ich brenne
> in dir; das Holz hat lange widerstrebt,
> der Flamme, die du loderst, zuzustimmen,
> nun aber nähr' ich dich und brenn in dir.
> Mein hiesig Mildsein wird in deinem Grimmen
> ein Grimm der Hölle nicht von hier.
> Ganz rein, ganz planlos frei von Zukunft stieg
> ich auf des Leidens wirren Scheiterhaufen,
> so sicher nirgends Künftiges zu kaufen
> um dieses Herz, darin der Vorrat schwieg.
> Bin ich es noch, der da unkenntlich brennt?
> Erinnerungen reiß ich nicht herein.
> O Leben, Leben: Draußensein.
> Und ich in Lohe. Niemand der mich kennt.

In Michael Hamburger's translation:[31]

> Now come, the last that I can recognize,
> Pain, utter pain, fierce in the body's texture.
> As once in the mind I burned, so now I burn
> In you; the wood resisted, long denied
> Acceptance to the flame you blazed at me,
> But now I feed you and in you I flare.
> My mildness here in your hot rage must turn
> Quite pure of forethought, futureless and free
> I mounted suffering's tangled, criss-cross pyre,
> so sure there was no purchase to acquire
> for this heart's future, all its store now silent.
> What burns there, so transmuted, is that I?
> Into this fire I drag no memory.
> To be alive, alive: to be outside.
> And I ablaze. With no one who knows me.

As for the epitaph, there are scores of studies, ranging not only through the whole of Rilke but through the whole tradition of rose-symbolism, that attempt to get behind these gnomic lines with their paradox of an anonymous identity that somehow includes the individual, like the poet with all his poems, and is yet indistinguishable from the totality of being.[32]

Orpheus. Eurydike. Hermes

Das war der Seelen wunderliches Bergwerk.
Wie stille Silbererze gingen sie
Als Adern durch sein Dunkel. Zwischen Wurzeln
entsprang das Blut, das fortgeht zu den Menschen,
und schwer wie Porphyr sah es aus im Dunkel.
Sonst war nichts Rotes.

Felsen waren da
und wesenlose Wälder. Brücken über Leeres
und jener große graue blinde Teich,
der über seinem fernen Grunde hing
wie Regenhimmel über einer Landschaft.
Und zwischen Wiesen, sanft und voller Langmut,
erschien des einen Weges blasser Streifen,
wie eine lange Bleiche hingelegt.

Und dieses einen Weges kamen sie.

Voran der schlanke Mann im blauen Mantel,
der stumm und ungeduldig vor sich aussah.
Ohne zu kauen fraß sein Schritt den Weg
in großen Bissen; seine Hände hingen
schwer und verschlossen aus dem Fall der Falten
und wußten nicht mehr von der leichten Leier,
die in die Linke eingewachsen war
wie Rosenranken in den Ast des Ölbaums.
Und seine Sinne waren wie entzweit;
indes der Blick ihm wie ein Hund vorauslief,
umkehrte, kam und immer wieder weit
und wartend an der nächsten Wendung stand, –
blieb sein Gehör wie ein Geruch zurück.
Manchmal erschien es ihm als reichte es

bis an das Gehen jener beiden andern,
die folgen sollten diesen ganzen Aufstieg.
Dann wieder wars nur seines Steigens Nachklang
und seines Mantels Wind was hinter ihm war.
Er aber sagte sich, sie kämen doch;
sagte es laut und hörte sich verhallen.
Sie kämen doch, nur wärens zwei
die furchtbar leise gingen. Dürfte er
sich einmal wenden (wäre das Zurückschaun
nicht die Zersetzung dieses ganzen Werkes,
das erst vollbracht wird), müßte er sie sehen,
die beiden Leisen, die ihm schweigend nachgehn:

Den Gott des Ganges und der weiten Botschaft,
die Reisehaube über hellen Augen,
den schlanken Stab hertragend vor dem Leibe
und flügelschlagend an den Fußgelenken;
und seiner linken Hand gegeben: *sie*.

Die So-geliebte, daß aus einer Leier
mehr Klage kam als je aus Klagefrauen;
daß eine Welt aus Klage ward, in der
alles noch einmal da war: Wald und Tal
und Weg und Ortschaft, Feld und Fluß und Tier;
und daß um diese Klage-Welt, ganz so
wie um die andre Erde, eine Sonne
und ein gestirnter stiller Himmel ging,
ein Klage-Himmel mit enstellten Sternen – :
Diese So-geliebte.

Sie aber ging an jenes Gottes Hand,
den Schritt beschränkt von langen Leichenbändern,
unsicher, sanft und ohne Ungeduld.
Sie war in sich, wie Eine hoher Hoffnung,
und dachte nicht des Mannes, der voranging,
und nicht des Weges, der ins Leben aufstieg.
Sie war in sich. Und ihr Gestorbensein
erfüllte sie wie Fülle.
Wie eine Frucht von Süßigkeit und Dunkel,
so war sie voll von ihrem großen Tode,
der also neu war, daß sie nichts begriff.

Sie war in einem neuen Mädchentum
und unberührbar; ihr Geschlecht war zu
wie eine junge Blume gegen Abend, und ihre Hände
waren der Vermählung
so sehr entwöhnt, daß selbst des leichten Gottes
unendlich leise, leitende Berührung
sie kränkte wie zu sehr Vertraulichkeit.

Sie war schon nicht mehr diese blonde Frau,
die in des Dichters Liedern manchmal anklang,
nicht mehr des breiten Bettes Duft und Eiland
und jenes Mannes Eigentum nicht mehr.

Sie war schon aufgelöst wie langes Haar
und hingegeben wie gefallner Regen
und ausgeteilt wie hundertfacher Vorrat.

Sie war schon Wurzel.

Und als plötzlich jäh
der Gott sie anhielt und mit Schmerz im Aufruf
die Worte sprach: Er hat sich umgewendet –,
begriff sie nichts und sagte leise: *Wer?*

Fern aber, dunkel vor dem klaren Ausgang,
stand irgend jemand, dessen Angesicht
nicht zu erkennen war. Er stand und sah,
wie auf dem Streifen eines Wiesenpfades
mit trauervollem Blick der Gott der Botschaft
sich schweigend wandte, der Gestalt zu folgen,
die schon zurückging dieses selben Weges,
den Schritt beschränkt von langen Leichenbändern,
unsicher, sanft und ohne Ungeduld.

In J. B. Leishman's translation:[33]

> That was the so unfathomed mine of souls.
> And they, like silent veins of silver ore,
> were winding through its darkness. Between roots
> welled up the blood that flows on to mankind,
> like blocks of heavy porphyr in the darkness.
> Else there was nothing red.

But there were rocks
and ghostly forests. Bridges over voidness
and that immense, grey, unreflecting pool
that hung above its so far distant bed
like a grey rainy sky above a landscape.
And between meadows, soft and full of patience,
appeared the pale strip of the single pathway,
like a long line of linen laid to bleach.

And on this single pathway they approached.

In front the slender man in the blue mantle,
gazing in dumb impatience straight before him.
His steps devoured the way in mighty chunks
they did not pause to chew; his hands were hanging,
heavy and clenched, out of the falling folds,
the lyre which had grown into his left
like twines of roses into a branch of olive.
It seemed as though his senses were divided:
for, while his sight ran like a dog before him,
turned round, came back, and stood, time and again,
distant and waiting, at the path's next turn,
his hearing lagged behind him like a smell.
It seemed to him at times as though it stretched
back to the progress of those other two
who should be following up this whole ascent.
Then once more there was nothing else behind him
but his climb's echo and his mantle's wind.
He, though, assured himself they still were coming;
said it aloud and heard it die away.
They still were coming, only they were two
that trod with fearful lightness. If he durst
but once look back (if only looking back
were not undoing of this whole enterprise
still to be done), he could not fail to see them, the two
light-footers, following him in silence:
The god of faring and of distant message,
the travelling-hood over his shining eyes,
the slender wand held out before his body,

the wings around his ankles lightly beating,
and in his left hand, as entrusted, *her.*

She, so belov'd, that from a single lyre
more mourning rose than from all women-mourners —
that a whole world of mourning rose, wherein
all things were once more present: wood and vale
and road and hamlet, field and stream and beast, —
and that around this world of mourning turned,
even as around the other earth, a sun
and a whole silent heaven full of stars,
a heaven of mourning with disfigured stars: —
she, so beloved.

But hand in hand now with that god she walked,
her paces circumscribed by lengthy shroudings,
uncertain, gentle, and without impatience.
Wrapt in herself, like one whose time is near,
she thought not of the man who went before them,
nor of the road ascending into life.
Wrapt in herself she wandered. And her deadness
was filling her like fulness.
Full as a fruit with sweetness and with darkness
was she with her great death, which was so new
that for the time she could take nothing in.

She had attained a new virginity
and was intangible; her sex had closed
like a young flower at the approach of evening,
and her pale hands had grown so disaccustomed
to being a wife, that even the slim god's
endlessly gentle contact as he led her
disturbed her like a too great intimacy.

Even now she was no longer that blonde woman
who'd sometimes echoed in the poet's poems,
no longer the broad couch's scent and island,
nor yonder man's possession any longer.

She was already loosened like long hair,
and given far and wide like fallen rain,
and dealt out like a manifold supply.

She was already root.

And when, abruptly,
the god had halted her and, with an anguished
outcry, outspoke the words: He has turned round! –
she took in nothing, and said softly: Who?

But in the distance, dark in the bright exit,
someone or other stood, whose countenance
was indistinguishable. Stood and saw
how, on a strip of pathway between meadows,
with sorrow on his look, the god of message
turned silently to go behind the figure
already going back by that same pathway,
its paces circumscribed by lengthy shroudings,
uncertain, gentle, and without impatience.

It is generally assumed that the poem, written at the beginning of 1904 in Rome, was occasioned by a classical relief of Orpheus, Eurydice and Hermes, based on a Greek original in marble, dating from about 420 B.C., which is lost, but of which there are three Roman copies from about the first or second centuries A.D., one in the Louvre, one in the Villa Albani in Rome, which may be the immediate occasion of the poem, and one in Naples. Rilke probably knew all three, certainly he speaks of the one in Naples, though that was after the poem was written. The relief captures the moment when Orpheus breaks his promise and Hermes Psychopompos is about to lead Eurydice back to Hades. Eurydice was veiled as she followed Orpheus and here Orpheus is lifting the veil, Eurydice has her hand on Orpheus' shoulder, they are gazing at each other, but Hermes is about to lead her away. The details of this classical representation are probably not very relevant to the poem, though one may remark in passing that those who do examine this aspect of the poem in detail come to quite different conclusions. Thus, Else Buddeberg, one of the main interpreters of Rilke generally and of this poem in particular, declares that, comparing the situation in the relief and in the poem, there is no correspondence of any kind.[34] Hans Berendt, on the other hand in his book on the *New Poems*, says with equal conviction: it is extraordinary how exactly the poet remembered the representation – one can only marvel at the precision of his vision and recall in the correspondence between plastic and poem.[35] Each critic seeks to prove the point by picking out different details. Else Buddeberg is more convincing, but perhaps the matter is not that important.

The first 15 lines give the setting of the poem in metaphorical form, the underworld as the "wondrous" mine of the souls. It is a landscape of shades, of the insubstantial and unreal, perhaps of forgetfulness, if the reference is to Lethe. But the metaphor of the silver-mines, followed through with the image of the veins, is altogether positive and paradoxically life-giving, for the world of the living has its roots in and is nourished from this underworld. So the setting already suggests that Rilke is giving a different sense of direction to the Orpheus/Eurydice story.

Next there is a long description of Orpheus, with the emphasis on his impatience, devouring the distance, like a hungry animal. The Orpheus of this poem, therefore, is totally different to, indeed the antithesis of the Orpheus of the later *Sonnets*. The Orpheus of the *Sonnets*, unlike the Orpheus here, is in the tradition of the ideal Orpheus, of art in all its purity. If in that tradition, in Boethius, for example, Eurydice represents the dark and desire-driven aspect that threatens the purity and detachment of Orpheus, here that dark desire is represented by Orpheus himself, whereas the *Sonnets* say of the song of Orpheus:

> Gesang, wie du ihn lehrst, ist nicht Begehr
>
> For song, as taught by you, is not desire.

Hence it is rather Eurydice here who prefigures the later Orpheus. This Orpheus is a distraught figure. If in Greek mythology Orpheus is in the end torn to pieces by the Maenads, this Orpheus is torn in himself, as suggested in the images of the senses, sight running ahead impatiently like a dog, hearing anxiously lagging behind, like a lingering aroma. Orpheus' gift and his power as a musician is recalled in the reference to his mourning music for Eurydice, an elegy so intense and a music so powerful that it is felt to create a whole new cosmos, recreating wood and vale, road and hamlet, stream and beast in an inner universe. But now he is oblivious even to his music in his concern with his mission – and in the sense of the poem it is a misguided mission, something not permitted, "unerlaubt", to use the word of the poem "Auferweckung des Lazarus", "The Raising of Lazarus", which depicts Christ unwillingly doing violence to nature, giving in to the people's lack of faith and their mistaken distinction between the living and the dead.

It is not Orpheus, however, or his action that is at the centre of Rilke's poem, but Eurydike and her state of mind. For both Ovid and Vergil the emphasis is on the undertaking and suffering of Orpheus, seen from the perspective of the living, but for Rilke the woman, not the man, is at the centre, and, instead of love-interest, the interest, from the otherworld perspective, is on the autonomy and otherness of Eurydike, away from possessiveness and invasion of privacy. If the emphasis in the case of Orpheus is on his impatience and on the way he is inwardly torn, in the case of Eurydice it is on her fulfillment, her wholeness, wrapt in herself and calm almost to the point of unconsciousness – one notes that it is twice said of her that she understood or took in nothing and one may speculate on the implications of that. There are many difficulties of detail, but it seems clear enough that the overall theme is not so much the bereavement of Orpheus as the fulfillment of Eurydike. In the end she has become absorbed in the landscape as described at the beginning. Her depiction concludes with the phrase: she was already root, and the preceding line: that she was distributed like hundredfold provision, echoes both *The Book of Hours* and the *Sonnets to Orpheus*, harks back to the image of dissemination in the death of St. Francis and anticipates the sentiment of what Rilke himself called the most valid of all the *Sonnets*, the 13th sonnet of the second part, which enjoins one to count oneself among the stock, the "Vorrat", in the fulness of nature.

How one responds to the idea is, perhaps, not the same thing as how one responds to the poem. One can marvel at the poem without being altogether convinced of its "truth". And whatever about its absolute truth, it is surely not true – nor is there any reason why it should be – to the classical original. There is nothing in Vergil or Ovid that would support the view of life, of death, that Rilke seems to be communicating here. Rilke's Eurydike knows no such nostalgic yearning for an earlier life as do the insubstantial and joyless shades of the Greek underworld. Odysseus reports how in the underworld he praised to his face the incomparable Achilles, who was honoured like a god in his lifetime and who now rules over the spirits, and so should have no regrets:

"No, do not repine in death, Achilles". So I spoke, but at once he answered: "Odysseus, do not gloss over death to me. I would rather be above ground still and labouring for some poor portionless man, than be lord over all the lifeless dead".[36]

Rilke's poem comes to a very different conclusion, ending with the return of Eurydike, which, in the context of the poem, is a return to her true self and more a triumph of Eurydike than a failure of Orpheus. Though, of course, Orpheus does fail and in her interpretation Else Buddeberg, speaking of that failure, says: is it for that reason that the last lines of the poem do not even name him any more?[37] Berendt understands that namelessness differently. He also draws attention to the way Orpheus is described at the end, dark and nameless, standing at the bright "Ausgang", which for Berendt is not only the "exit" but the "outcome". He points out that Orpheus no longer laments, no longer attempts to pursue the beloved. Orpheus, too, he concludes, has come to acquiesce in the reality of death, has become transformed into a god-like figure, for that is how, as a mark of awe, Berendt understands the namelessness of Orpheus at the end.[38] Buddeberg's reading seems more convincing than the idea of Orpheus' sudden conversion. But one's response to the poem does not, in the end, depend on arguments about Rilke's ideas. Considered in terms of its ideas, the poem does seem far removed from the pathos of the original myth. It is quite possible, however, that concentration on the ideas blunts one's response to the imagery and melody, the emotional evocativeness of the poem's dramatic narrative. In a more immediate reading of the poem the narrative of loss and grief, underlined and, as it were, sanctified by the anguished cry of the god Hermes, is still strongly present in spite of Rilke's idiosyncratic ideas and partisanship.

Finally one may note the biographical background to this poem. Throughout his life Rilke insisted on the need for solitude as the *sine qua non* of development and creativity. It is perhaps the most persistent of all themes in his letters and for obvious reasons it was a particularly urgent matter at the time of the poem, in the early years of his marriage. And one remembers too that other marriage, of Paula Becker and Otto Modersohn and Rilke's later requiem, with its oddly inverted version of the Eurydice story. The correspondence between Paula Modersohn-Becker's story and Rilke's "Orpheus. Eurydike. Hermes" is remarkable. Reference was made already to Otto Modersohn's letters to his wife, reminding her of her duty to return. In Paula Modersohn-Becker's volume of letters and diaries we find her saying of those same letters:

> Wenn Ottos Briefe zu mir kommen, so sind sie
> wie eine Stimme von der Erde, und ich selbst bin
> wie eine, die gestorben ist und in seligen
> Gefilden weilt und diesen Erdenschrei hört.[39]

Naturally one does not want to over-emphasise the biographical element, the problems of Rilke's own marriage or of analogous situations in his circle, reducing the poem to an argument *pro domo*. Still one can hardly ignore the biographical context altogether.

Duino Elegies

Before coming to the *Sonnets* it is necessary to consider briefly the *Elegies*, not so much because most people, certainly Rilke himself, regarded them as his main work, but because the *Sonnets* arose in the context of the *Elegies'* composition. It is important, however, not to to allow a guide to the *Sonnets* to be side-tracked into an interpretation of the *Elegies*. Accordingly these prefatory remarks are kept to a minimum and do not claim even to be concerned with what is most important in the *Elegies* themselves, but relate to what seems to be most useful for the reader of the *Sonnets* to know beforehand about the *Elegies* and about what Rilke himself said regarding them.

The first Elegy: "Wer, wenn ich schriee, hörte mich denn ...", "Who, if I cried, would hear me ...", sets the tone of the whole work in the sense of isolation and insecurity, homelessness and transitoriness. Yet it ends on a hopeful note and with a myth that echoes the myth of Orpheus. In a reversal of Nietzsche, the final five lines suggest the birth of music out of the spirit of tragedy:

> Ist die Sage umsonst, daß einst in der Klage um Linos
> wagende erste Musik dürre Erstarrung durchdrang;
> daß erst im erschrockenen Raum, dem ein beinah
>   göttlicher Jüngling
> plötzlich für immer enttrat, das Leere in jene
> Schwingung geriet, die uns jetzt hinreißt und tröstet
>   und hilft.

> Is the story in vain, how once, in the mourning for Linos,
> venturing earliest music pierced barren numbness, and how,
> in the startled space an almost deified youth
> suddenly quitted for ever, emptiness first
> felt the vibration that now charms us and comforts
> and helps?[40]

The reference is to the myths surrounding Linos, variously identified, in the classical tradition, as a poet who died young and is mourned by his father, Apollo, or as himself a god of nature worship, the lament for him being a dirge of the departing summer. Or again he is credited with the invention of music or said to have been the teacher of Orpheus. The lament for Linos is mentioned, for example, by Homer in the *Iliad* as a scene on the shield of Achilles, Homer's description giving the sense in which music transforms the melancholy of lament:[41]

> Girls and young men, innocent-hearted, were carrying out the honey-sweet crop in woven baskets. In their midst a boy was playing a lovely tune on a clear-sounding lyre and to it sweetly singing the Linos-song in his delicate voice: they followed him with singing and shouting, and danced behind him with their feet beating time to his music.

The whole cycle ends on a rising note with the affirmation of lament in the Tenth Elegy – the one most specifically concerned with death and the world of the dead – with its "Landscape of Lamentation" contrasted with the garish distraction and fair-ground noise that seeks to conceal the presence of death. This affirmation of death, which in one sense might seem a pious and religious attitude, is one of the main criticisms levelled against Rilke's ideas by one of his most engaged critics and interpreters of the *Elegies*, the cultural historian, Romano Guardini, from whose theological stand-point death is not something to be affirmed, but something from which to be redeemed.[42]

All of the *Elegies* are relevant to the *Sonnets*, but the Ninth Elegy is the one that most obviously gives an answer and a sense of purpose to the elegiac situation, elaborating on that "Auftrag", that mission or task given to man, already referred to in the First Elegy. There is a danger in so emphasising the Ninth Elegy, as if the poet were answering problems rather than giving expression to questionings. However, when Rilke himself sets about explaining the *Elegies*, it is that "Auftrag" he particularly concentrates on.

The Ninth Elegy, then, asks once more why, if the condition is so singularly and painfully transitory, why we have to be human, and suggests that it is in the experience, the consciousness of being the most fleeting of all that we find our purpose in naming and preserving all the transitory things around us –

> Sind wir vielleicht *hier,* um zu sagen: Haus,
> Brücke, Brunnen, Tor, Krug, Obstbaum, Fenster ...

> Are we, perhaps, *here* just for saying: House,
> Bridge, Fountain, Gate, Jug, Fruit tree, Window ...

– transforming them into the inwardness of ourselves

> in – o unendlich – in uns! wer wir am Ende auch seien,

> into – oh, endlessly – into ourselves! Whosoever we are

– a significantly tentative eschatological phrase. The Ninth Elegy concludes:

> Erde, ist es nicht dies, was du willst: unsichtbar
> in uns erstehn? – Ist es dein Traum nicht,
> einmal unsichtbar zu sein? – Erde! unsichtbar!
> Was, wenn Verwandlung nicht, ist dein drängender
>   Auftrag?
> Erde, du liebe, ich will. Oh glaub, es bedürfte
> nicht deiner Frühlinge mehr, mich dir zu gewinnen –,
>   *einer,*
> ach, ein einziger ist schon dem Blute zu viel.

Namenlos bin ich zu dir entschlossen, von weit her.
Immer warst du im Recht, und dein heiliger Einfall
ist der vertrauliche Tod.
Siehe, ich lebe. Woraus? Weder Kindheit noch Zukunft
werden weniger ... Überzähliges Dasein
entspringt mir im Herzen.

Earth, is it not just this that you want: to arise
invisibly in us? Is not your dream
to be one day invisible? Earth! invisible!
What is your urgent command, if not transformation?
Earth, you darling, I will! Oh, believe me, you need
no more of your spring-times to win me over: a single
  one,
ah, one, is already more than my blood can endure.
Beyond all names I am yours, and have been for ages.
You were always right, and your holiest inspiration
is Death, that friendly Death.
Look, I am living. On what? Neither childhood nor future
are growing less ... Supernumerous existence
wells up in my heart.

This supernumerous existence, related to Rilke's almost obsessive prejudice against all notions of counting and numbering – a sign, some would say, of Rilke's irrationalism – this superfluity of life is something that Rilke will then celebrate over and over in the *Sonnets*, as in the opening of the 22nd Sonnet of the second part:

O trotz Schicksal: die herrlichen Überflüsse
unseres Daseins,

Oh, but in spite of fate,
life's glorious abundance.

Rilke's own main commentary on the *Elegies* is the long letter he wrote to his Polish translator, Witold von Hulewicz, explaining the *Elegies* in terms of the great unity of existence and of that "Auftrag", the function of man to remain so open to and absorbent of life as to transform the transitory and visible into an invisible and abiding inwardness. It must be said that this aspect of the *Elegies*, though so much emphasised by Rilke, does not greatly appeal to some critics. In his edition of the *Elegies* Stahl says:[43]

> This development of the theme of invisibility at the end of the ninth elegy has met with the greatest amount of incomprehesion and disapproval from Rilke critics.

Those critics, like Schwarz,[44] most concerned with Rilke's sociological content, or lack of it, tend to reject such an unpolitical myth of inwardness, though one could equally argue that its function in Rilke's poetry is to find a purposeful direction beyond aesthetic self-containment and contentment with the work of art as an end in itself. Or again, coming to Rilke from a different angle, this idea of man's mission is no less deplored by a critic like Bassermann, who is perhaps the most passionate Rilke disciple among the critics, but for whom Rilke – his "other Rilke" i.e. not the Rilke of Rilke's pious congregation – is the poet of humanity's lonely heroism, his poetry enshrining the tragic dignity of man with total abandon.[45] He rejects any myth of redemption, whether by way of religion or of art, so that for him that "Auftrag" can only be an aberration, an unfortunate attempt by Rilke to evade his own elegiac insight. One may sympathise with Bassermann, but he does seem to ignore too much that is in Rilke from beginning to end. For all the sense of anxiety and exposure in Rilke, there is no Benn-like suggestion in him that the work of art is merely an erratic artifact and unhistorical, vouchsafing the cold comfort of itself, but permitting no other comforting deductions from the aesthetic orders and satisfactions of the mind. It is an axiom of the poetic experience as Rilke speaks of it, that the very nature of poetry is felt to be mysteriously affirmative, just as he says of rhyme that it is a great goddess, the divinity of ancient and secret coincidences, not a means of poetry, but an infinitely affirmative yes.[46] Rilke had gone steadily along the path already indicated in the early diaries, when he said:

> Wie andere ferne Welten zu Göttern reifen werden – weiß ich nicht. Aber für uns ist die Kunst der Weg ...[47]

The kind of godless conclusion devoutly wished for by Bassermann is just not in Rilke, certainly not admitted, and his world really is, or at any rate claims to be "full of relationships". So the idea of the "Auftrag" in the *Elegies* is no sudden construction, nor can it be extracted as an idea to be pronounced on in isolation. It derives its validity and its force from the artistic experience in Rilke's life, which is also the material in his work, though in a more than private sense and with a more than personal purposefulness, extending the experience of rhyme and rhythm, pattern and order to a whole world-view of *telos* and *logos* and *cosmos*.

Hulewicz had sent a questionnaire to Rilke, and Rilke replies with regard to the *Elegies*:[48]

> Lebens- und Todesbejahung erweist sich als Eines in den "Elegien". Wir müssen versuchen, das größeste Bewußtsein unseres Daseins zu leisten, das in beiden unabgegrenzten Bereichen zu Hause ist, aus beiden unerschöpflich genährt ... es gibt weder ein Diesseits noch Jenseits, sondern die große Einheit ... Wir, diese Hiesigen und Heutigen, sind nicht einen Augenblick in der Zeitwelt befriedigt, noch in sie gebunden; wir gehen immerfort über und über zu den Früheren, zu unserer Herkunft und zu denen, die scheinbar nach uns kommen ... Die Vergänglichkeit stürzt überall in ein tiefes Sein. Und so sind alle Gestaltungen des Hiesigen nicht nur zeitbegrenzt zu gebrauchen, sondern, soweit wirs vermögen, in jene überlegenen Bedeutungen einzustellen, an denen wir Teil haben.

Aber nicht im christlichen Sinne, (von dem ich mich immer leidenschaftlicher entferne), sondern in einem rein irdischen, tief irdischen, selig irdischen Bewußtsein gilt es, das h i e r Geschaute und Berührte in den weiteren, den weitesten Umkreis einzuführen. Nicht in ein Jenseits, dessen Schatten die Erde verfinstert, sondern in ein Ganzes, in das Ganze ... unsere Aufgabe ist es, diese vorläufige, hinfällige Erde uns so tief, so leidend und leidenschaftlich einzuprägen, daß ihr Wesen in uns "unsichtbar" wieder aufersteht. Wir sind die Bienen des Unsichtbaren. Nous butinons éperdument le miel du visible, pour l'accumuler dans la grande ruche d'or de l'Invisible. Die Elegien zeigen uns an diesem Werke, am Werke dieser fortwährenden Umsetzungen des geliebten Sichtbaren und Greifbaren in die unsichtbare Schwingung und Erregtheit unserer Natur ... Wenn man den Fehler begeht, katholische Begriffe des Todes, des Jenseits und der Ewigkeit an die Elegien oder Sonette zu halten, so entfernt man sich völlig von ihrem Ausgang und bereitet sich ein immer gründlicheres Mißverstehen vor. Der "Engel" der Elegien hat nichts mit dem Engel des christlichen Himmels zu tun (eher mit den Engelgestalten des Islam) ... Der Engel der Elegien ist dasjenige Geschöpf, in dem die Verwandlung des Sichtbaren in Unsichtbares, die wir leisten, schon vollzogen erscheint.

In conclusion Rilke says of the coming together of *Elegies* and *Sonnets*:

Elegien und Sonette unterstützen einander beständig, und ich sehe eine unendliche Gnade darin, daß ich, mit dem gleichen Atem, diese beiden Segel füllen durfte: das kleine rostfarbene Segel der Sonette und der Elegien riesiges weißes Segel-Tuch.

The *Elegies* and *Sonnets* complement each other. The sense of a universe full of relationships is more dominant in the *Sonnets*, whereas the *Elegies* mainly convey that sense of being outside and opposite that is particularly the theme of the Eighth Elegy:

> Dieses heißt Schicksal: gegenüber sein
> und nichts als das und immer gegenüber.

> For this is Destiny: being opposite,
> and nothing else, and always opposite.

That Elegy concludes with the lines:

> Wer hat uns also umgedreht, daß wir,
> was wir auch tun, in jener Haltung sind
> von einem, welcher fortgeht? Wie er auf
> dem letztem Hügel, der ihm ganz sein Tal
> noch einmal zeigt, sich wendet, anhält, weilt –,
> so leben wir und nehmen immer Abschied.

> Who's turned us round like this, so that we always,
> do what we may, retain the attitude
> of someone who's departing? Just as he,
> on the last hill, that shows him all his valley
> for the last time, will turn and stop and linger,
> we live our lives, for ever taking leave.

The same motifs occur in *Elegies* and *Sonnets*, but with different resonances. The motif of breathing, for example, is in the *Sonnets* associated with relationships, with interaction and intercourse, whereas in the *Elegies* it was mainly a motif of transitoriness, as in the Second Elegy:

> Denn wir, wo wir fühlen, verflüchtigen; ach wir
> atmen uns aus und dahin

> For we, when we feel, evaporate; oh, we
> breathe ourselves out and away.

The "cry", with which the *Elegies* so stridently begin, announcing the theme of human disorder, is, as implied in the last, the 26th Sonnet of the first part, "outsounded with orphic order". Similarly the 26th Sonnet of the second part invokes the singing god who "orders the criers". But it was because he had the experience of writing the *Elegies* that he was able to come to this sense of order in the *Sonnets*. It does seem as if in the end his constant concern is his own experience of poetic creativity. Doubtless there is a narcissistic element in this, but the experience is presented as something that points beyond itself. Hence the story of the composition of the *Elegies*, so dramatically reported in Rilke's letters, is not just source-material about their genesis, but concerns their substance, based as this is on the assumption that that experience of art which gave meaning to his life had a more than private reference.

The *Sonnets to Orpheus*

In contrast to the ten years of agonised and often despairing effort in the composition of the *Elegies*, these 55 *Sonnets* were composed – or Rilke would like to think: dictated to him – with apparent effortlessness between the 2nd and 23rd February 1922. They are called sonnets, but apart from the regular number of lines, there is little else regular about them. A few are in regular iambic pentameters. Some are mainly in trochaic pentameters. But mostly they are in mixed trochaic and dactylic lines of very varied length, from two feet to seven feet. The rhythm constantly changes and there is no formal metrical structure. Rilke had observed earlier that his translations of old Italian sonnets had convinced him how appropriate still was this form, which afforded an "almost heightened freedom" within its "most demanding restriction".[49] Immediately after the composition of the *Sonnets* he wrote to Katharina Kippenberg:[50]

> Ich sage immerzu Sonette. Ob es gleich das Freieste, sozusagen Abgewandelste wäre, was sich unter dieser, sonst so stillen and stabilen Form begreifen ließe. Aber gerade dies: das Sonett abzuwandeln, es zu heben, ja gewissermaßen es im Laufen zu tragen, ohne es zu zerstören, war mir, in diesem Fall, eine eigentümliche Probe und Aufgabe: zu der ich mich, nebenbei, kaum zu entscheiden hatte. So sehr war sie gestellt und trug ihre Lösung in sich.

The orphic theme was nothing new in Rilke, but the immediate occasion seems to have been an Italian drawing from around 1500 of Orpheus making music in the forest. One of Rilke's last and most passionate love affairs was with a painter, Baladine Klossowska, whom he called Merline. The affair followed the usual pattern, some ecstatic weeks, followed by a long troubled period, on Rilke's side not without recrimination and even revulsion. In any case, Merline, on one of her visits to Muzot, had pinned a postcard over Rilke's desk, a copy of a pen-and-ink drawing by Cima da Conegliano depicting Orpheus making music under a tree and being listened to by the birds and beasts of the forest. Earlier, for Christmas 1920, she had given him a present of a Latin-French edition of Ovid's *Metamorphosis*. A second occasion for the *Sonnets* was the account of a young girl's death. According to the dedication, they were written as a monument for a young dancer who had died as a teenager a few years before and about whose life and death Rilke had recently learned from the letters of her mother to him. Only a couple of the *Sonnets* have direct reference to her. She may be regarded as a Eurydike figure, though now the emphasis is less on loss and lament, than on celebration, celebration of the orphic music that was at home and effective both in the here-and-now and in the underworld and through which, Rilke believes, we can be open to death as to life and experience existence as altogether praiseworthy. The *Sonnets* are variations on all the familiar Rilke themes, with Orpheus as the presiding genius, and since Orpheus represents music, art, poetry itself, one can relate Orpheus or aspects of the orphic myth to any one of the 55 poems, though only a minority of the poems invoke the figure of Orpheus or have any direct reference to the orphic myth.

ERSTER TEIL Track 77

I

Da stieg ein Baum. O reine Übersteigung!
O Orpheus singt! O hoher Baum im Ohr!
Und alles schwieg. Doch selbst in der Verschweigung
ging neuer Anfang, Wink und Wandlung vor.

Tiere aus Stille drangen aus dem klaren
gelösten Wald von Lager und Genist;
und da ergab sich, daß sie nicht aus List
und nicht aus Angst in sich so leise waren,

sondern aus Hören. Brüllen, Schrei, Geröhr
schien klein in ihren Herzen. Und wo eben
kaum eine Hütte war, dies zu empfangen,

ein Unterschlupf aus dunkelstem Verlangen
mit einem Zugang, dessen Pfosten beben, –
da schufst du ihnen Tempel im Gehör.

The sonnet begins in an exclamatory, startling manner with the image of the tall tree in the ear. Like any of the sonnets it can be analysed *ad infinitum* and almost any line, image, word can be annotated, if only by tracing its history in the rest of Rilke. But this would be to lose the immediacy and blunt the impact. Whatever its complexity, one can say that the subject-matter of the sonnet is simply the song of Orpheus and its effect. It draws obviously from mythological tradition, in particular Ovid's description of the trees gathering around Orpheus. But Rilke makes of this a very inward event, something that takes place within the sense of hearing. Orpheus is the transformer, creating a new life for what was small and meagre, obscure and anxious. Rilke uses the term "Wandlung" for this transformation and one remembers his Catholic upbringing and that "Wandlung" is the term for consecration at the Mass. It is a sacred transformation and where before there were anxious refuges, now there are temples. "Übersteigung" at the beginning signals a transcendence. In music we transcend ourselves. In the Seventh Elegy the same term is used, where the poet, or man, is proudly showing to the angel the achievements of humanity, the great cathedrals, for example, or even more, music:

> Chartres war groß –, und Musik
> reichte noch weiter hinan und überstieg uns.
>
> Chartres was great – and music
> towered still higher and passed beyond us.

The same term occurs in the poem called "An die Musik", "To Music", the theme of which is the otherness, the beyond-comprehension nature of music, something that is innermost and so most remote from the surface of our lives. There Music is addressed as:

> our innermost, transcending and reaching beyond us
>
> Innigstes unser,
> das, uns übersteigend, hinausdrängt.

II

Und fast ein Mädchen wars und ging hervor
aus diesem einigen Glück von Sang und Leier
und glänzte klar durch ihre Frühlingsschleier
und machte sich ein Bett in meinem Ohr.

Und schlief in mir. Und alles war ihr Schlaf.
Die Bäume, die ich je bewundert, diese
fühlbare Ferne, die gefühlte Wiese
und jedes Staunen, das mich selbst betraf.

Sie schlief die Welt. Singender Gott, wie hast
du sie vollendet, daß sie nicht begehrte,
erst wach zu sein? Sieh, sie erstand und schlief.

> Wo ist ihr Tod? O, wirst du dies Motiv
> erfinden noch, eh sich dein Lied verzehrte? –
> Wo sinkt sie hin aus mir? ... Ein Mädchen fast ...

The theme of this sonnet, too, is the creative power of orphic song, but adding a new element to the familiar features of the Orpheus story. Now Orpheus' creation is referred to as a girl. One possible source for the image of the inner girl is that in the anthropology of Rilke's time there was much discussion of androgyny and related matters. In particular Rilke knew and had attended lectures by Alfred Schuler, who spoke about the complementary sexuality present in everybody, about the artist in whose innermost being man and woman embrace and whose work of art brings to life what slumbers within like a sleeping beauty. In a letter to Clara, Rilke suggests that the *Sonnets* may owe much to his contact with Schuler.[51] But there are precedents in Rilke himself. In that *Turning-point* poem already referred to he exhorted himself to:

> do heart-work
> on all the images imprisoned within you
> ... See, inner man, thy inner woman.

> Werk des Gesichts ist getan
> tue nun Herz-Werk
> an den Bildern in dir, jenen gefangenen ...
> Siehe, innerer Mann, dein inneres Mädchen...

"The deepest experience of the creative artist is feminine", he wrote in an early letter: "das tiefste Erleben des Schaffenden ist weiblich".[52]

This inner woman, creation of the singing god, is referred to as sleeping. Sleep, up to his famous epitaph, is in Rilke something to be immortalised and celebrated. Hostile Rilke critics relate this to Rilke's distrust of the all too wakeful – they would say: of the rational, he would say: of the all too detached and divisive. He constantly champions an "open" attitude, absorbent and totally absorbed, it might seem to the point of unselfconscious identification. Of course there is a paradox here, in this very conscious celebration of sleep, just as there is a paradox in the epitaph's "nobody's sleep" under the name Rainer Maria Rilke. But taken on Rilke's own terms this orphic creation, this sleeper, recreating our whole world, is open to the whole of life and so surely to death also. Hence the questions with which the sonnet ends and which one can take to be addressed to Orpheus or as Rilke questioning himself and his ability to include the most difficult of all motifs. But apart from the implied resolve to include death in any affirmation of life, one doubts if any answers about death are implied in these final questions. In the most detailed commentary on the *Sonnets to Orpheus* Mörchen would seem to argue that there is here an acceptance of annihilation, that orphic song itself will not survive, that it will expire, be consumed. But taking Rilke's work as a whole, one can only be certain of his intention, as he says in his letters was the intention of the *Elegies*, to "keep life open towards death". In the last, the Tenth Elegy, the one most concerned with that motif, there is, in contrast to the true elegiac landscape, a very bitter picture of false living in an extended image of the noisy fair-ground:

> ... beklebt mit Plakaten des "Todlos",
> jenes bitteren Biers, das den Trinkenden süß scheint,
> wenn sie immer dazu frische Zerstreuungen kaun...

> ... plastered with placards for "Deathless",
> that bitter beer that tastes quite sweet to its drinkers
> so long as they chew with it plenty of fresh
>   distractions ...

The closing question – can the orphic song include even death? – can be understood as addressed to the poet himself. But essentially the first two sonnets centre on Orpheus, whereas the third turns to the difficulties of the human poet as he seeks to follow in the footsteps of the singing god.

III

Ein Gott vermags. Wie aber, sag mir, soll
ein Mann ihm folgen durch die schmale Leier?
Sein Sinn ist Zwiespalt. An der Kreuzung zweier
Herzwege steht kein Tempel für Apoll.

Gesang, wie du ihn lehrst, ist nicht Begehr,
nicht Werbung um ein endlich noch Erreichtes;
Gesang ist Dasein. Für den Gott ein Leichtes.
Wann aber *sind* wir? Und wann wendet *er*

an unser Sein die Erde und die Sterne?
Dies *ists* nicht, Jüngling, daß du liebst, wenn auch
die Stimme dann den Mund dir aufstößt, – lerne

vergessen, daß du aufsangst. Das verrinnt.
In Wahrheit singen, ist ein andrer Hauch.
Ein Hauch um nichts. Ein Wehn im Gott. Ein Wind.

Rilke refers throughout to Orpheus as a god, though that is not in the ancient tradition of the orphic myth. The theme here is the discordant nature of man as contrasted with the purity of true existence and therefore of true music, like that of the singing god. (If this is related, in part, to the theme of the incompatibility of art and life, one cannot help remembering Rilke's at this time increasingly troubled relationship with Baladine Klossowska.) Apollo, the god of art and song, of brightness, is not the god of the complexities, of the crossroads of human relationships. Crossroads seem to have traditionally negative associations. In classical antiquity the sanctuaries that stood at crossroads were to the less benevolent gods, who had to be placated. One may well find something inhuman in this attitude towards human relationships and there is in Rilke a mistrust, not just of personal involvements, but of the human condition as contrasted with the rest of creation. This is a persistent attitude, a mistrust of humanity as persistent as the celebration of life. Circumstances like the Great War confirmed his feeling. Writing to Sophie Liebknecht in 1917, he agrees that the world, life may well be beautiful, but, he goes on:

> alas, not humanity ... its madness is a prison for us, and the fact of being human has set us outside the whole of nature in its unity.[53]

> Nature is happy. In us there is a confusion of warring forces.

> Natur ist glücklich. Doch in uns begegnen
> sich zuviel Kräfte, die sich wirr bestreiten ...[54]

In the definitions come to here as a consequence of this ideal of the uncomplicatedly natural there may seem to be something negative and even nihilistic. Song is existence and true singing is "a breath about nothing", "ein Hauch um nichts". But this ideal of being as the rest of creation is an old and persistent theme in Rilke. In a letter to Clara, in the context of a discussion of art's non-selective affirmation as exemplified by Cézanne, he had said:

> in the end, all we have to do is to be there, but simply, fervently, as the earth is there.

> Wir haben im Grunde nur dazusein, aber schlicht, aber inständig, wie die Erde da ist.[55]

True singing, this sonnet suggests, would have the simplicity and intensity of a natural phenomenon. It is, to be sure, strange that, in opposition to that song that is desire, "Begehr", and that will pass away, "verrinnt", the ideal put forward as contrast is a breath, a breath about nothing. However one responds to this, it is clear that for Rilke this nothing, this nowhere being-there, is not negatively meant. In that eighth elegy which has as its theme the contrast between man, enclosed in his life of desire, and the openness of the rest of creation, we read of this "nowhere without no":

> *Wir* haben nie, nicht einen einzigen Tag,
> den reinen Raum vor uns, in den die Blumen
> unendlich aufgehn, Immer ist es Welt
> und niemals Nirgends ohne Nicht: das Reine,
> Unüberwachte, das man atmet und
> unendlich *weiß* und nicht begehrt.

> We've never, no, not for a single day,
> pure space before us, such as that which flowers
> endlessly open into; always world,
> and never nowhere without no: that pure,
> unsuperintended element one breathes,
> endlessly knows, and never craves.

Is this an inhuman ideal or something like an *unio mystica*, this final definition of song as a breath about nothing, a gust in the god, a wind? Probably one is on safest ground if one relates it once more to poetry and poetic creativity as Rilke claimed to experience it – and for Rilke it was undoubtedly a religious experience, a Pentecostal "powerful wind from heaven". He experienced it most powerfully in the case of the *Elegies*, where the inspiration is described to Princess Marie as a nameless storm, a hurricane in the spirit, "ein namenloser Sturm, ein Orkan im Geist".[56]

IV

O ihr Zärtlichen, tretet zuweilen
in den Atem, der euch nicht meint,
laßt ihn an eueren Wangen sich teilen,
hinter euch zittert er, wieder vereint.

O ihr Seligen, o ihr Heilen,
die ihr der Anfang der Herzen scheint.
Bogen der Pfeile und Ziele von Pfeilen,
ewiger glänzt euer Lächeln verweint.

Fürchtet euch nicht zu leiden, die Schwere,
gebt sie zurück an der Erde Gewicht;
schwer sind die Berge, schwer sind die Meere.

Selbst die als Kinder ihr pflanztet, die Bäume,
wurden zu schwer längst; ihr trüget sie nicht.
Aber die Lüfte ... aber die Räume ...

A sonnet addressed, Leishman suggests, "aux jeunes filles en fleurs". It would appear to encompass two spheres: both the world of the young lovers, which is a world of bliss and of pain, with the traditional imagery of Cupid's arrow, of which the lover is at once impetus and target, and, continuing the breath imagery of the preceding sonnet, the "other world", heedless of us, of the air outside. The sonnet takes the form of a double exhortation, on the one hand to accept the heaviness and suffering of the life that attaches us to the earth, but also to follow Orpheus in "overstepping" into the other world outside of us, that does not mean us and that, it is implied at the end, does not have the heaviness of the world to which we are attached. The ending is enigmatic and nowhere is that other world, to which one must gain entry if one is to survive, more delicately invoked than in the opening image of the "breath that does not mean you". But it accords with the ethical trend of the whole cycle, which suggests survival only in a wholeness that transcends the self.

V

Errichtet keinen Denkstein. Laßt die Rose
nur jedes Jahr zu seinen Gunsten blühn.
Denn Orpheus ists. Seine Metamorphose
in dem und dem. Wir sollen uns nicht mühn

um andre Namen. Ein für alle Male
ists Orpheus, wenn es singt. Er kommt und geht.
Ists nicht schon viel, wenn er die Rosenschale
um ein paar Tage manchmal übersteht?

O wie er schwinden muß, daß ihrs begrifft!
Und wenn ihm selbst auch bangte, daß er schwände.
Indem sein Wort das Hiersein übertrifft,

> ist er schon dort, wohin ihrs nicht begleitet.
> Der Leier Gitter zwängt ihm nicht die Hände.
> Und er gehorcht, indem er überschreitet.

The idea that poets through the ages are the one poet is an early and persistent theme in Rilke. Behind all poems there is one poet, says a character in an early play[57] and in 1920 Rilke says: "Kunst kann nur aus rein anonymer Mitte hervorgehen".[58] In another letter from the same year we read:

> ... Denn im letzten Sinne giebt es nur Einen, jenen Unendlichen, der sich da und dort durch die Zeiten in einem, ihm unterworfenen Geiste geltend macht.[59]

The name for this metamorphic poet is here Orpheus, a name now used by Rilke much as he had earlier used the name of God. Rilke seems to be giving, as it were once for all, a definition of his Orpheus when he says here:

> Ein für alle Male
> ists Orpheus, wenn es singt

translated by Leishmann as:

> Once and for all,
> it's Orpheus when there's song

and by Mitchell as:

> It is Orpheus once for all
> whenever there is song

– translations which do not quite get across the identification, in the German "it sings", of the music of Orpheus with the harmony, rhythm and rightness of existence. So even the name Orpheus is a name for anonymity, for poetry, art, is, like birdsong singing the seasons, an anonymous one praising the anonymous, as it is put in the little dedicatory poem beginning "There loves a heart", "Es liebt ein Herz": "Ein Anonymes preist das Anonyme, /wie Vogelaufruf das Gefühl des Jahrs ..." Rilke commits himself up to the end, up to the epitaph, to this namelessness, a promise of "nameless devotion" solemnly made at the end of the Ninth Elegy, where he says to the earth: "Namenlos bin ich zu dir entschlossen".

There is, to be sure, something odd about this insistence on an art that should be totally impersonal and anonymous in the case of a body of poetry so idiosyncratic as Rilke's. The same applies to the secondary literature, which tends to involve the personal story of the poet more rather than less than in the case of other poets. Some, like Michael Hamburger, would see this as a reason why Rilke's reputation might suffer. Knowing, for example, that the third sonnet here may have behind it the troubled relationship with Baladine Klossowska may seem, while going some way to explain it, also to debase it. Rilke himself is very insistent that relating the work of art to the artist is not the proper approach, that indeed nothing is more urgent, as he puts it, than to direct attention away from the person of the artist.[60] For good or ill, readers and critics are not likely to follow his advice.

In this sonnet, then, Orpheus is the name and mythical image for all poetry and poets. But one may note finally the sense in which Orpheus, as well as image, is also model and exemplar, namely in his obedience to metamorphosis and to the laws of this life that is for ever changing, passing over and away. He, too, must pass, fade, "schwinden". The Ninth Elegy had referred to man as "Uns, die Schwindendsten", "Us, the most fleeting of all", and the First Elegy had evoked the strange world of shades and namelessness:

> Freilich ist es seltsam, die Erde nicht mehr zu bewohnen,
> /.../
> das, was man war in unendlich ängstlichen Händen,
> nicht mehr zu sein, und selbst den eigenen Namen
> =wegzulassen wie ein zerbrochenes Spielzeug.

> True, it is strange to inhabit the earth no longer,
> /.../
> to be no longer all that one used to be
> in endlessly anxious hands, and to lay aside
> even one's proper name like a broken toy.

In the sonnet we are called upon to understand that Orpheus, too, must "pass over" or "pass away", however we wish to translate "schwinden", "überschreiten" – and of course between "over" and "away" there may be a world of difference. In his interpretation of the sonnet, Mörchen would see the Orpheus myth in Rilke as precisely in opposition to any idea of survival.

> Orpheus is primal mythical image, not as one who lasts, but as one who fades.

> Nicht als der Dauernde, sondern als der Schwindende ist Orpheus mythisches Urbild.

And Mörchen goes on: only in so far as he renounces name, fame, commemorating stone, can the singer be the metamorphosis of Orpheus. This may be a logical reading of the sonnet, but on the question of survival and permanence, as on so many other matters, Rilke would seem more agnostic than anything else. Probably one cannot pin him down to anything more definite than, for example, when he says in a letter at the end of 1920:

> Längst hab ich mich ja gewöhnt, die gegebenen Dinge nach ihrer Intensität aufzufassen, ohne, soweit das menschlich leistbar ist, um die Dauer besorgt zu sein, – es ist am Ende die beste und diskreteste Art, ihnen alles zuzumuten –, selbt die Dauer.[61]

In any case the emphasis here seems to me to be much less on fading or not surviving than on Orpheus "transcending by transgressing", overstepping the divide between life and death, just as the Orpheus of Vergil, through his singing, crossed over the divide between life and death.

VI

Ist er ein Hiesiger? Nein, aus beiden
Reichen erwuchs seine weite Natur.
Kundiger böge die Zweige der Weiden,
wer die Wurzeln der Weiden erfuhr.

Geht ihr zu Bette, so laßt auf dem Tische
Brot nicht und Milch nicht; die Toten ziehts –.
Aber er, der Beschwörende, mische
unter der Milde des Augenlids

ihre Erscheinung in alles Geschaute;
und der Zauber von Erdrauch und Raute
sei ihm so wahr wie der klarste Bezug.

Nichts kann das gültige Bild ihm verschlimmern;
sei es aus Gräbern, sei es aus Zimmern,
rühme er Fingerring, Spange und Krug.

Continuing the theme of the preceding sonnet, and like the Orpheus of Vergil, who, by the power of his music, crosses over the divide between the living and the dead, Orpheus is said here to encompass the "whole", the whole of life, root and branch, to be at home in both realms, in this and the other world. The sonnet both celebrates the overstepping of Orpheus and exhorts us not to separate those worlds, as if the other world had to be lured by magic, but, like Orpheus, to see and celebrate the intermingling of otherworldly apparition with ordinary observation, the identity of the magical and the mundane, the natural and the supernatural, the rooms of the living and the graves of the dead, the furniture of one or of the other.

VII

Rühmen, das ists! Ein zum Rühmen Bestellter,
ging er hervor wie das Erz aus des Steins
Schweigen. Sein Herz, o vergängliche Kelter
eines den Menschen unendlichen Weins.

Nie versagt ihm die Stimme am Staube,
wenn ihm das göttliche Beispiel ergreift.
Alles wird Weinberg, alles wird Traube,
in seinem fühlenden Süden gereift.

Nicht in den Grüften der Könige Moder
straft ihm die Rühmung Lügen, oder
daß von den Göttern ein Schatten fällt.

Er ist einer der bleibenden Boten,
der noch weit in die Türen der Toten
Schalen mit rühmlichen Früchten hält.

A relatively simple poem, celebrating Orpheus, or the nameless poet, as one who praises and whose praise is unfailing and undeterred by darkness and death. The opening image is of the bell, cast from the ore of the earth and giving it a voice.

Praise is one of the most prominent motifs in Rilke and especially praise as the function of the artist, the most obvious expression being the often-anthologised dedicatory poem:

> Oh sage, Dichter, was du tust? – Ich rühme
>
> O tell me, poet, what you do? I praise,

the phrase "I praise" being the refrain of that poem. As with much else in Rilke, one can view it as a religious motif and in particular see it in the biblical tradition of praise as the divinely ordained function of man, "praising for ever and ever" in the words of the Psalms. As in the case of the *Stundenbuch*, Rilke continues to draw on and take his resonance from the Christian tradition. But if it is fair to note this, it is necessary also to counterbalance it by noting, for example, one of the most important prose documents of Rilke's later period, composed precisely in the days in which he was composing the Fifth and Tenth Elegies, indeed written in the same copybook. This is the so-called *Der Brief des jungen Arbeiters*, The Letter of a Young Workman, a fictional letter, supposedly written by a working-class admirer to the Belgian writer Verhaeren. It is an angry letter of accusation against what he sees as a repressive Christianity, particularly in its distortion of sexuality and its neglect of life on earth. The sonnet can be read in the spirit of that letter, which ends with the final plea:

> Gebt uns Lehrer, die uns das Hiesige rühmen. Sie sind ein solcher.
>
> Give us teachers, who will praise for us the here and now. You are such a one.[62]

VIII

Nur im Raum der Rühmung darf die Klage
gehn, die Nymphe des geweinten Quells,
wachend über unserm Niederschlage,
daß er klar sei an demselben Fels,

der die Tore trägt und die Altäre. –
Sieh, um ihre stillen Schultern früht
das Gefühl, daß sie die jüngste wäre
unter den Geschwistern im Gemüt.

Jubel *weiß* und Sehnsucht ist geständig, –
nur die Klage lernt noch; mädchenhändig
zählt sie nächtelang das alte Schlimme.

Aber plötzlich, schräg und ungeübt,
hält sie doch ein Sternbild unsrer Stimme
in den Himmel, den ihr Hauch nicht trübt.

The sonnet continues the praise-theme and expresses one of Rilke's deepest convictions, that the elegiac must end, like the *Elegies* themselves with the Tenth, with praise and celebration. As he says in one of his more depressed periods, in a letter from Toledo:

> ... ich bin gerade jetzt mehr als je im Einseitigen, die Klage hat vielfach überwogen, aber ich weiß, man darf die Klagesaiten nur dann so ausführlich gebrauchen, wenn man entschlossen ist, auf ihnen, mit ihren Mitteln, später auch den ganzen Jubel zu spielen, der hinter jedem Schweren, Schmerzhaften und Ertragenen anwächst und ohne den die Stimmen nicht vollzählig sind.[63]

The song of Orpheus himself arises out of lamentation. But, this sonnet implies, lamentation is a preliminary, apprentice mood-mode, compared with the older mood-sisters of jubilation or yearning. The image is that of the nymph telling beads of the sorrowful mysteries, guarding the purities of sorrow's precipitation, sensing her own youth and yet suddenly, albeit inexpertly and indirectly, producing a pure, unclouded constellation. The specific reference is doubtless to the nymph Byblis, whose story is told in Book 9 of Ovid – her passion for her brother leads her to dissolve in tears and "beyond death she reappears as a spring", as Malte relates.[64] In dedicatory verses for Ellen Key in 1909 Rilke had recalled the myths of Byblis and Daphne, metamorphoses of the eternal lovers, and in a letter to Sidonie Nádherny he suggests that the place of the artist can only be at such a spring, at such a dark daphnean laurel.[65]

IX

Nur wer die Leier schon hob
auch unter Schatten,
darf das unendliche Lob
ahnend erstatten.

Nur wer mit Toten vom Mohn
aß, von dem ihren,
wird nicht den leisesten Ton
wieder verlieren.

Mag auch die Spieglung im Teich
oft uns verschwimmen:
Wisse das Bild.

Erst in dem Doppelbereich
werden die Stimmen
ewig und mild.

A complementary sonnet to the preceding one. If lamentation is only proper as a prelude to jubilation, that jubilation itself is only proper to those who have sung in the shadows beforehand. Once again it is a sonnet presided over by Orpheus, as the one who is both here and beyond, who played also for the shades. Only by including death, by partaking of communion with the dead, only by inhabiting the double realm of the beyond–here do we catch our own fleeting reflection, do we know ourselves. The underlined "Wisse das Bild" is the Know Thyself at the heart of the poem.

X T86

Euch, die ihr nie mein Gefühl verließt,
grüß ich, antikische Sarkophage,
die das fröhliche Wasser römischer Tage
als ein wandelndes Lied durchfließt.

Oder jene so offenen, wie das Aug
eines frohen erwachenden Hirten,
– innen voll Stille und Bienensaug –
denen entzückte Falter entschwirrten;

alle, die man dem Zweifel entreißt,
grüß ich, die wiedergeöffneten Munde,
die schon wußten, was Schweigen heißt.

Wissen wirs, Freunde, wissen wirs nicht?
Beides bildet die zögernde Stunde
in dem menschlichen Angesicht.

A sonnet centred on the Roman sarcophagi, which had long served as watering troughs, as aqueducts, on which Rilke had written the poem "Römische Sarkophage" and about which he often speaks. According to Rilke himself: "In der zweiten Strophe ist gedacht der Gräber in dem berühmten alten Friedhof der Allyscamps bei Arles, von dem auch im *Malte Laurids Brigge* die Rede ist".[66] In *Malte* it is said of the Prodigal Son:

> Soll ich ihn sehen im seelengewohnten Schatten der Allyscamps, wie sein Blick zwischen den Gräbern, die offen sind wie die Gräber Auferstandener, eine Libelle verfolgt?[67]

Welcoming these symbols of life-in-death, Rilke is welcoming all who, having known doubt and death, having known silence, have regained the power of speech – but then, in an unusual address to his fellow-men, asks himself and us if we do indeed have knowledge, and concludes that the human countenance is characterised by a hesitancy between knowing and not knowing. We live in a twilit condition. The hesitancy and uncertainty is built into the last lines, where it is impossible to say which is subject, "Beides" or "die zögernde Stunde". Once again, though, it is clear that the theme is the orphic double-realm of life and death and one thinks of the music of Orpheus when it is said here that the life-giving water flows through the sarcophagi "like a wandering song".

XI

Sieh den Himmel. Heißt kein Sternbild "Reiter"?
Denn dies ist uns seltsam eingeprägt:
dieser Stolz aus Erde. Und ein Zweiter,
der ihn treibt und hält und den er trägt.

Ist nicht so, gejagt und dann gebändigt,
diese sehnige Natur des Seins?
Weg und Wendung. Doch ein Druck verständigt.
Neue Weite. Und die zwei sind eins.

Aber *sind* sie's? Oder meinen beide
nicht den Weg, den sie zusammen tun?
Namenlos schon trennt sie Tisch und Weide.

Auch die sternische Verbindung trügt.
Doch uns freue eine Weile nun
der Figur zu glauben. Das genügt.

This puzzling sonnet seems at first remote from the Orpheus theme. Several commentators point out that Mizar, the middle star of the handle of The Plough and the little star Alco that lies above it were known to the Arabs as The Horse and Rider.[68] But even if we assume that Rilke takes the image, as again in the Tenth Elegy, from there, that does not explain its significance here. Leishman suggests:

> Human nature might be symbolized by a horse, and "the god", the unseen power that uses it, directs it, rides it, and to which – we must believe – it should willingly submit, by a rider.

But it would seem more likely that horse and rider together are an image of human life and that the sonnet is once again on the theme of human disunity. We wish to be united with nature, with the proud earth, and sometimes feel so, searching the heavens for a sign of that union in a constellation. But in reality we are as separated from nature as the animal's pasture is from the table. The constellation deceives in the sense that, as the Fourth Elegy says, we are never at one, "einig". Yet the sonnet ends with the "sufficiency" of believing for a while in that sign, that figure or symbol, a belief that gladdens us. Taken by itself, with no reference to the rest of Rilke, this might suggest an attitude to art, to its symbols and images on the lines of Benn's "Artistik", as something that does indeed gladden the human heart, but only as a life-enhancing lie. But Rilke has none of this mistrust of art or of the imagination, though he may well be accused of mistrusting man's more critical and rational faculties. Any constellation or "Figur" that would symbolise human harmoniousness would be deceptive, albeit true in the larger context, in the harmony of "the whole". In dedicatory verses that Rilke wrote for Hans Carossa he puts his faith in "the enduring realm of transformation", which gives form to our lives, even to our losings and forgettings. We may be rarely at the centre of life's circles, but the whole and healing "figure" is drawn around us:

> Auch noch Verlieren ist unser; und selbst das Vergessen
> hat noch Gestalt in dem bleibenden Reich der
> Verwandlung. Losgelassenes kreist; und sind wir auch
> selten die Mitte einem der Kreise: sie ziehn um uns die
> heile Figur.[69]

We may be disunited in our daily lives, but, as the next sonnet suggests, it is in the realm of the "symbol" that our true life is lived.

XII

Heil dem Geist, der uns verbinden mag;
denn wir leben wahrhaft in Figuren.
Und mit kleinen Schritten gehn die Uhren
neben unserm eigentlichen Tag.

Ohne unsern wahren Platz zu kennen,
handeln wir aus wirklichem Bezug.
Die Antennen fühlen die Antennen,
und die leere Ferne trug ...

Reine Spannung. O Musik der Kräfte!
Ist nicht durch die läßlichen Geschäfte
jede Störung von dir abgelenkt?

Selbst wenn sich der Bauer sorgt und handelt,
wo die Saat in Sommer sich verwandelt,
reicht er niemals hin. Die Erde *schenkt*.

The sonnet "hails the spirit that can unify us", celebrates that orphic harmony of the whole that is full of relationships and serves to bind, even unbeknown to us. As so often in Rilke, there is a mistrust of man's knowingness, even of the most "natural" conscious activity, like the work of the farmer. The true source is rather the earth itself. What we have in life is rather earth's gift than something we have consciously arrived at. One could say that the abiding ideal of the *Sonnets* is to feel truly united with the whole of earthly existence, an ideal which this sonnet suggests is ever and again realised, albeit unknowingly. Even the very fact that we are so busy with the trivial occupations of our daily round serves to ensure that, being otherwise occupied, we do not interrupt the flow of relationships, the "music of forces" that fill the spaces of that real life-time, that "figurative" world in which we "truly live", that accompanies our daily clock-round.

XIII

Voller Apfel, Birne und Banane,
Stachelbeere ... Alles dieses spricht
Tod und Leben in den Mund ... Ich ahne ...
Lest es einem Kind vom Angesicht,

wenn es sie erschmeckt. Dies kommt von weit.
Wird euch langsam namenlos im Munde?
Wo sonst Worte waren fließen Funde,
aus dem Fruchtfleisch überrascht befreit.

Wagt zu sagen, was ihr Apfel nennt.
Diese Süße, die sich erst verdichtet,
um, im Schmecken leise aufgerichtet,

klar zu werden, wach und transparent,
doppeldeutig, sonnig, erdig, hiesig –:
O Erfahrung, Fühlung, Freude –, riesig!

A sonnet that is emphatically earthy and sensuous, but in a way that includes the ineffability and mystery of "namelessness" and the double-meaning of the "double-realm". In a strange prose-fragment of 1919, *Ur-Geräusch*, Primal Sound, Rilke combines recollections of phonograph experiments at school with later studies of anatomy and speculates on the "primal sound" that might be heard, if one were to track the coronal suture rather than the grooves of a cylinder. There he speaks of the widening of horizons that might come if the artist were to develop an ever more nimble and ever more spiritual fingering with the "five-fingered hand of his senses".[70] This sonnet, like – still more obviously perhaps ("dance the orange") – the fifteenth sonnet, attempts to convey such a sensuous experience and suggests that a total experience of the fruit would be an experience of the totality of earthly existence, which is both emphatically "here", "hiesig", and ineffably "from afar", "von weit", and which includes death as all living things do.

XIV

Wir gehen um mit Blume, Weinblatt, Frucht.
Sie sprechen nicht die Sprache nur des Jahres.
Aus Dunkel steigt ein buntes Offenbares
und hat vielleicht den Glanz der Eifersucht

der Toten an sich, die die Erde stärken.
Was wissen wir von ihrem Teil an dem?
Es ist seit lange ihre Art, den Lehm
mit ihrem freien Marke zu durchmärken.

Nun fragt sich nur: tun sie es gern? ...
Drängt diese Frucht, ein Werk von schweren Sklaven,
geballt zu uns empor, zu ihren Herrn?

Sind *sie* die Herrn, die bei den Wurzeln schlafen,
und gönnen uns aus ihren Überflüssen
dies Zwischending aus stummer Kraft und Küssen?

The idea of the great unity, the inclusion in the here and now of the underworld or other-world, is one of the most emphasised aspects of Rilke's belief and one of the main reasons for the choice of the Orpheus myth. But if there is insistence on this inclusion, there is no claim to knowledge of the dead and there is a certain scepticism, even irony, in the question here: are they sullen slaves or are they magnanimous lords? But the main image is of a world above nourished by an underworld, as the fruits of the earth have their roots in the darkness beneath.

XV

Wartet ..., das schmeckt ... Schon ists auf der Flucht.
... Wenig Musik nur, ein Stampfen, ein Summen –:
Mädchen, ihr warmen, Mädchen, ihr stummen,
tanzt den Geschmack der erfahrenen Frucht!

Tanzt die Orange. Wer kann sie vergessen,
wie sie, ertrinkend in sich, sich wehrt
wider ihr Süßsein. Ihr habt sie besessen.
Sie hat sich köstlich zu euch bekehrt.

Tanzt die Orange. Die wärmere Landschaft,
werft sie aus euch, daß die reife erstrahle
in Lüften der Heimat! Erglühte, enthüllt

Düfte um Düfte. Schafft die Verwandtschaft
mit der reinen, sich weigernden Schale,
mit dem Saft, der die Glückliche füllt!

With its dactylic rhythm the sonnet is an exhortation to dance the taste of the experienced fruit, to so completely experience the fruits of the earth, the earth itself, as to live it, to absorb it into one's being, into one's own body. The relationship to "the whole" is expressed in a graphic, even erotic manner, bringing together the attributes of the fruit, its warmth and fragrance, its sweetness, ripeness and smoothness with the figure of the dancing girls, into whom the fruit has been "converted" – it is hardly accidental that Rilke here again uses a religious term, for he is proposing a "religion" to replace what he feels to be an earth-denying Christianity.

XVI

Du, mein Freund, bist einsam, weil ...
Wir machen mit Worten und Fingerzeigen
uns allmählich die Welt zu eigen,
vielleicht ihren schwächsten, gefährlichsten Teil.

Wer zeigt mit Fingern auf einen Geruch? –
Doch von den Kräften, die uns bedrohten,
fühlst du viele ... Du kennst die Toten,
und du erschrickst vor dem Zauberspruch.

Sieh, nun heißt es zusammen ertragen
Stückwerk und Teile, als sei es das Ganze.
Dir helfen, wird schwer sein. Vor allem: pflanze

mich nicht in dein Herz. Ich wüchse zu schnell.
Doch *meines* Herrn Hand will ich führen und sagen:
Hier. Das ist Esau in seinem Fell.

The sonnet is addressed to a dog, as Rilke explains.[71] Several letters refer to his affinity with dogs. Asked in his later life about influences, he first passes the obvious names in review, from Jacobsen to Cézanne, but then wonders if it is not the quieter things that have essentially influenced his formation, giving contact with a dog as his first example.[72] Dogs are what he understands best, they are for him the most human, he wrote to Pricess Marie,[73] and in that letter to the Princess in which he speaks most openly of his "almost furious anti-Christianity", his own "religiosity" is exemplified in a scene from his time in Cordoba:

> ... wo eine kleine häßliche Hündin, im höchsten Grade vormutterschaftlich, zu mir kam; es war kein rühmliches Tier, und sicher war sie voll zufälliger Junge, von denen kein Aufhebens gemacht worden

sein wird; aber sie kam, da wir ganz allein waren, so
schwer es ihr fiel, zu mir herüber und hob ihre von
Sorge und Innerlichkeit vergrößerten Augen auf und
begehrte meinen Blick, – und in dem ihren war
wahrhaftig alles, was über den Einzelnen hinausgeht,
ich weiß nicht wohin, in die Zukunft oder ins
Unbegreifliche; es löste sich so, daß sie ein Stück
Zucker von meinem Kaffee abbekam, aber nebenbei, o
so nebenbei, wir lasen gewissermaßen die Messe
zusammen, die Handlung war an sich nichts als
Geben und Annehmen, aber der Sinn und der Ernst
und unsere ganze Verständigung war grenzenlos. Das
kann doch nur auf Erden geschehen, es ist auf alle
Fälle gut, hier willig durchgegangen zu sein, wenn
auch unsicher, wenn auch schuldig, wenn auch ganz
und gar nicht heldenhaft, – man wird am Ende
wunderbar auf göttliche Verhältnisse vorbereitet
sein.[74]

Knowing how fanatically he protects his own solitude, one is not surprised that he declines to look after a friend's dog, giving as his reason precisely his feeling of infinite affinity with dogs and his response to their heart-breaking dependence, which would lead him to break off, bit by bit like dog-biscuits, pieces of his heart.[75] The argument is not specious, if convenient.

In the sonnet the affinity of man and dog leads to a reflection on our fragmentary hold on the world, our common attempt to comprehend the world as a whole. Compared to the loneliness of the dog, we seem, albeit without the animal's keen sense of smell, to be more at home in the world by means of words and gestures. Yet our condition is similar and our task is the same, to make a whole out of our fragmentary experience. The last lines are the most puzzling. Withdrawing, as Rilke did in reality, from too close an involvement, with the suggestion perhaps, not only that the human partner would sacrifice too much of himself, but that the life of the animal would be overpowered and stifled, the poet offers instead to act as mediator between God and animal. For once Rilke explains the last lines in a letter to Countess Sizzo:

> In dem Gedicht *an den Hund* ist unter "meines Herrn Hand" die Hand des Gottes gemeint; hier des "Orpheus". Der Dichter will diese Hand führen, daß sie auch, um seiner unendlichen Teilnehmung und Hingabe willen, den Hund segne, der, fast wie Esau, sein Fell auch nur umgetan hat, um in seinem Herzen einer ihm nicht zukommenden Erbschaft: des ganzen menschlichen Not und Glück, teilhaft zu werden.[76]

It may be that Rilke confuses here Jacob and Esau, but in any case the meaning seems to be that the poet invokes the blessing of Orpheus on the friend of man, the animal that most closely shares man's condition and aspiration.

XVII

Zu unterst der Alte, verworrn,
all der Erbauten
Wurzel, verborgener Born,
den sie nie schauten.

Sturmhelm und Jägerhorn,
Spruch von Ergrauten,
Männer im Bruderzorn,
Frauen wie Lauten ...

Drängender Zweig an Zweig,
nirgends ein freier ...
Einer! O steig ... o steig ...

Aber sie brechen noch.
Dieser erst oben doch
biegt sich zur Leier.

This is a very deliberate and dense variation on the Orpheus theme of the inclusion of the other-world, the underworld of darkness and death, in the here and now. The image is of humanity's family tree, culminating in the music, the bent branch of the lyre at the top, but drawing its sustenance from its tangled roots, beginning with the source, the original Ancient, through all the history of warriors and women, a history of struggles and defeats, but finally emerging into the freedom and openness of music. Leisi suggests that Rilke may have taken the image of the Ancient's family-tree from the visionary dream of Booz, the ancestor of David in the Book of Ruth, in Victor Hugo's poem *Booz endormi*.[77]

XVIII 794

Hörst du das Neue, Herr,
dröhnen und beben?
Kommen Verkündiger,
die es erheben.

Zwar ist kein Hören heil
in dem Durchtobtsein,
doch der Maschinenteil
will jetzt gelobt sein.

Sieh, die Maschine:
wie sie sich wälzt und rächt
und uns entstellt und schwächt.

Hat sie aus uns auch Kraft,
sie, ohne Leidenschaft,
treibe und diene.

There is, as one might expect, much aversion in Rilke against the machine, as being at once hectic and heartless. He exchanges views, for example, with Katharina Kippenberg on the "sinfulness" of the machine, on the machine as humanity's misfortune, "Unheil".[78] In practice, too, Rilke preferred to avoid technology, writing *Elegies* and *Sonnets* by candle-light or oil-lamp in Muzot. It is a trait in Rilke that is often criticised. Demetz, for example, speaks of Rilke's "almost unqualified denial" of the machine.[79] Nevertheless, in line with his creed of all-inclusiveness, Rilke must also include the realities of the present age in his affirmation, and so, just as the worker in the so-called workman-letter speaks of bringing, as an offering to God, his work and his machine, as in the past the shepherd brought the lamb or the fruits of the field, in this sonnet the machine, for all its menace and for all that it threatens to drown the quietude, asserts its right to be praised. The Master addressed is Orpheus and the sonnet can be understood as an appeal to Orpheus to tame the machine as he once tamed man and beast.

XIX

Wandelt sich rasch auch die Welt
wie Wolkengestalten,
alles Vollendete fällt
heim zum Uralten.

Über dem Wandel und Gang,
weiter und freier,
währt noch dein Vor-Gesang,
Gott mit der Leier.

Nicht sind die Leiden erkannt,
nicht ist die Liebe gelernt,
und was im Tod uns entfernt,

ist nicht entschleiert.
Einzig das Lied überm Land
heiligt und feiert.

A sonnet directly celebrating orphic song as the only constant in a changing world. The first four lines of the sestet echo a famous passage in *Malte* that humanity has so far understood so little of what matters, of love, suffering, death.[80]

In the end one can only have recourse to the origin of song, to Orpheus' song-prelude. A kind of credo sonnet, therefore, in that it puts complete trust in song, in a musicality and mastery reflected here in the peculiar melodiousness and rhythmical flow of the sonnet. As in all of Rilke, it is not art as escape or for art's sake, but a confession of faith in the saving grace of art, in which the landscape of man is sanctified and celebrated.

XX

Dir aber, Herr, o was weih ich dir, sag,
der das Ohr den Geschöpfen gelehrt? –
Mein Erinnern an einen Frühlingstag,
seinen Abend, in Rußland –, ein Pferd ...

Herüber vom Dorf kam der Schimmel allein,
an der vorderen Fessel den Pflock,
um die Nacht auf den Wiesen allein zu sein;
wie schlug seiner Mähne Gelock

an den Hals im Takte des Übermuts,
bei dem grob gehemmten Galopp.
Wie sprangen die Quellen des Rossebluts!

Der fühlte die Weiten, und ob!
der sang und der hörte –, dein Sagenkreis
war *in* ihm geschlossen.
                      Sein Bild: ich weih's.

The poet addresses his master, Orpheus, who taught all creatures to hear, and wonders what offering he can bring him. Then he offers this memory of the horse in Russia. It is an "Ex-voto for Orpheus", as he says to Lou, reminding her of the time when this white horse came bounding up to them in a Volga meadow.[81] The horse is a creature full of orphic energy, singing and listening, and Rilke's letter to Lou tells of his own joy in the sudden, unexpected re-creation of an earlier experience, giving him the feeling of the overcoming of time. (The reader may or may not agree with the K.A. editors, who suggest that the galloping horse, with the picket at its foot, may represent Rilke's votive offering of gratitude after the "blocked" years before 1922.[82] It may indeed also be said to be analogous to that "freedom in constraint" to which Rilke, speaking of the sonnet form, referred.)

XXI

Frühling ist wiedergekommen. Die Erde
ist wie ein Kind, das Gedichte weiß;
viele, o viele ... Für die Beschwerde
langen Lernens bekommt sie den Preis.

Streng war ihr Lehrer. Wir mochten das Weiße
an dem Barte des alten Manns.
Nun, wie das Grüne, das Blaue heiße,
dürfen wir fragen: sie kanns, sie kanns!

Erde, die frei hat, du glückliche, spiele
nun mit den Kindern. Wir wollen dich fangen,
fröhliche Erde. Dem Frohsten gelingts.

O, was der Lehrer sie lehrte, das Viele
und was gedruckt steht in Wurzeln und langen
schwierigen Stämmen: sie singts, sie singts!

A relatively simple poem and with no direct reference to Orpheus, though a variation on the basic theme of celebration of the earth. To this "Spring-Children's-Song", "Frühlings-Kinder-Lied", as Rilke calls it – and which he refers to as the "brightest spring-sound" of the *Sonnets* – he exceptionally published a note, noting its association in his mind with the dancing melody in the singing of school-children, to the music of tambourine and triangle, he had heard at a morning

Mass in a little convent church in Spain.[83] The dancing rhythm finds its equivalent, then, in the predominantly dactylic metrical form. Spring gets to know the blue of the heavens or the green of growth like colours or lessons it has learned. Given the basic comparison between Spring released from winter, the teacher with the white beard, and the children released from school, there are no great difficulties in the poem and the details are clear enough, like the catching games or the word-play on stems and roots with their reference to school subjects and problems in language learning or mathematics.

Childhood had always been one of Rilke's main themes. Some critics indeed would hold against him that he so often favours the childish attitude as against the critical and reasoning world of the adult. It is certainly true that Rilke celebrates a child world that he often suggests is rudely interrupted by the returning and encroaching adult. One recalls again the eighth elegy and its theme of man's divisive and being-opposite attitude, unable to be completely open and absorbed. In the Leishman/Spender translation:

> We've never, no, not for a single day,
> pure space before us, such as that which flowers
> endlessly open into: always world,
> and never nowhere without no: that pure,
> unsuperintended element one breathes,
> endlessly knows, and never craves. A child
> sometimes gets quietly lost there, to be always
> jogged back again.

XXII

Wir sind die Treibenden.
Aber den Schritt der Zeit,
nehmt ihn als Kleinigkeit
im immer Bleibenden.

Alles das Eilende
wird schon vorüber sein;
denn das Verweilende
erst weiht uns ein.

Knaben, o werft den Mut
nicht in die Schnelligkeit,
nicht in den Flugversuch.

Alles ist ausgeruht:
Dunkel und Helligkeit,
Blume und Buch.

A Wordsworthian warning against haste, in favour of abiding values. Or one could also say: an echo of Stifter's gentle law, what matters and survives is what is quiet and restful, not a restfulness that is static or exclusive, but an enduring balance, like the balance of light and darkness.

XXIII

O erst *dann*, wenn der Flug
nicht mehr um seinetwillen
wird in den Himmelstillen
steigen, sich selber genug,

um in lichten Profilen,
als das Gerät, das gelang,
Liebling der Winde zu spielen,
sicher, schwenkend und schlank, –

erst, wenn ein reines Wohin
wachsender Apparate
Knabenstolz überwiegt,

wird, überstürzt von Gewinn,
jener den Fernen Genahte
sein, was er einsam erfliegt.

Flying is here representative of the modern technological world and the danger of its self-sufficiency. Only in relation to a goal and a whole can something truly be in a state of existence, such as is emphasised, not merely typographically, but in the striking one-sentence structure of the sonnet, with its single movement directed towards and culminating in that "sein".

XXIV

Sollen wir unsere uralte Freundschaft, die großen
niemals werbenden Götter, weil sie der harte
Stahl, den wir streng erzogen, nicht kennt, verstoßen
oder sie plötzlich suchen auf einer Karte?

Diese gewaltigen Freunde, die uns die Toten
nehmen, rühren nirgends an unsere Räder.
Unsere Gastmähler haben wir weit –, unsere Bäder,
fortgerückt, und ihre uns lang schon zu langsamen
    Boten

überholen wir immer. Einsamer nun auf einander
ganz angewiesen, ohne einander zu kennen,
führen wir nicht mehr die Pfade als schöne Mäander,

sondern als Grade. Nur noch in Dampfkesseln brennen
die einstigen Feuer und heben die Hämmer, die immer
größern. Wir aber nehmen an Kraft ab, wie Schwimmer.

Of the several sonnets specifically concerned with the modern world this is perhaps the most effective, if also – whatever significance may be attached to that – the most pessimistic, being a sonnet on the Hölderlin theme of a world devoid of divinity. Our "Gastmähler" and "Bäder" are no longer ritual feasts and ablutions, and the steam-boilers of the present have replaced the sacred fires of the past. We do not have the patience to await the messengers of the gods, rush straight ahead and no longer linger in "lovely meanders". So we are thrown back on ourselves and depend on one another at the same time that we are estranged from one another, not any more in common communion. The sonnet ends with a graphic final image of dwindling power: "But we are like swimmers whose strength is going".

XXV

Dich aber will ich nun, *Dich,* die ich kannte
wie eine Blume, von der ich den Namen nicht weiß,
noch *ein* Mal erinnern und ihnen zeigen, Entwandte,
schöne Gespielin des unüberwindlichen Schrei's.

Tänzerin erst, die plötzlich, den Körper voll Zögern,
anhielt, als göß man ihr Jungsein in Erz;
trauernd und lauschend –. Da, von den hohen Vermögern
fiel ihr Musik in das veränderte Herz.

Nah war die Krankheit. Schon von den Schatten bemächtigt,
drängte verdunkelt das Blut, doch, wie flüchtig verdächtigt,
trieb es in seinen natürlichen Frühling hervor.

Wieder und wieder, von Dunkel und Sturz unterbrochen,
glänzte es irdisch. Bis es nach schrecklichem Pochen
trat in das trostlos offene Tor.

This is the sonnet on the young girl to whom the work is dedicated. Like the whole cycle, she is the radiant counterpart to the elegiac, "the beautiful playmate of the invincible cry". In her life she progressed from dance to an ever more inward and mysterious music, until she is completely overshadowed and finally enters the underworld. Wherever Rilke wrote of her the aspect he emphasises most is her innocent openness to the whole of that great life-and-death unity. In his most elaborate articulation of the ideal of openness, of the great unity and life-and-death affirmation, in the letter to Hulewicz, he speaks of the *Sonnets* as a work in the name and under the protection of a dead girl, whose innocence held the door of the grave open, who is one of those forces that keep life open to the other wound-open half.[84]

And shortly before the *Sonnets* were composed, he had written to Vera's mother on the girl's unique sense of one-ness, on her affinity:

> mit dieser Einheit der seienden und während Welt, diese Zusage ans Leben, dieses freudige, dieses gerührte, dieses bis ins Letzte fähige Hineingehören ins Hiesige – ach, ins Hiesige nur?! Nein ... ins Ganze, in ein viel mehr als Hiesiges. Oh, wie, wie liebte sie, wie reichte sie mit den Antennen ihres Herzens über alles hier Erfaßliche und Umfängliche hinaus ...[85]

Like so much in Rilke, this is not so much difficult to understand as a difficult faith to follow. But he is very uncompromising. Doubtless the most striking word in this sonnet is the "trostlos" of the last line and it is an example of the necessity to understand Rilke on his own terms. In his context "Trost" has decidedly negative connotations and one has only to turn to the last Elegy to see his bitterness against what he feels are false consolations, like Christian doctrine, and to realise that the pejorative term in Rilke is not "trostlos" but "todlos", the denial and exclusion of death.

A Rilkean motto, suggesting that all attempts to console are troubled and murky, is "aller Trost ist trübe", a phrase from his letter "on the Feast of the Epiphany" 1923 to Countess Sizzo after the death of her mother.[86]

This is Rilke's most elaborate letter of condolence, in which "Trost" is dismissed as a fruitless distraction and in which he stresses over and over the unity of life and death. The ancient initiation into the mysteries must have meant the mysterious union of opposites, of light and darkness, sleep and wakefulness. We must learn to read the word death without negation, recover our unsuspecting trust, our "argloses Vertrauen". It is an uncompromising letter of condolence and Rilke himself seems to realise the difficulty of adhering to this creed. Death is the true yes-sayer, "der eigentliche Ja-Sager", he says at the end of the letter, adding in parentheses: "I implore you to believe it!". The "trostlos" of the twenty-fifth Sonnet is to be read in this context. It is probably impossible to convey this sense in translation, whatever term is used – most usually "hopelessly" (Leishman, Young, Paulin, Norton). Examples of other translations, probably more misleading are "desolate" (MacIntyre) or "unrelenting" (Norris/Keele).[87]

XXVI

Du aber, Göttlicher, du, bis zuletzt noch Ertöner,
da ihn der Schwarm der verschmähten Mänaden befiel,
hast ihr Geschrei übertönt mit Ordnung, du Schöner,
aus den Zerstörenden stieg dein erbauendes Spiel.

Keine war da, daß sie Haupt dir und Leier zerstör.
Wie sie auch rangen und rasten, und alle die scharfen
Steine, die sie nach deinem Herzen warfen,
wurden zu Sanftem an dir und begabt mit Gehör.

Schließlich zerschlugen sie dich, von der Rache gehetzt,
während dein Klang noch in Löwen und Felsen verweilte
und in den Bäumen und Vögeln. Dort singst du noch jetzt.

O du verlorener Gott! Du unendliche Spur!
Nur weil dich reißend zuletzt die Feindschaft verteilte,
sind wir die Hörenden jetzt und ein Mund der Natur.

The last sonnet of the first part returns to the figure of Orpheus and makes the most direct and detailed use of the Orpheus story, the story of his death. In the classical tradition there are several different accounts. The different versions agree that he was killed by enraged women, torn to pieces, apart from his head and his lyre, which were carried by the currents of the sea to Lesbos. Where the versions differ is in the motive for his killing, some accounts having more to do with religious rites, some with human jealousy. Orpheus, according to some, after his journey to Hades, had deserted the worship of Dionysus, chosen Apollo and the sun as his god and so aroused the anger of the maenads, the followers of Dionysus. In other accounts, Orpheus, out of grief after the loss of Eurydike, becomes a woman-hater. Rilke speaks of the scorned maenads. But these details are less essential. What matters for Rilke is the necessity of Orpheus' death and the survival of his song, for which we and the whole earth are audience, even the very stones that are hurled at him. The theme would seem to be: song and the order of Orpheus comes out of the suffering caused by human enmity – for while that enmity or hostility, "Feindschaft", is here that of the maenads, it is in Rilke generally characteristic of man, as in the fourth elegy: "Feindschaft / ist uns das Nächste", in the Leishman and Spender translation: "Hostility's our first response".

The sonnet ends:

> Only because enmity finally rent and dispersed
> you are we now hearers and a mouth of nature.

If the hostility of man dismembers and disperses the god Orpheus and if out of this dispersal or distribution, "Verteilung", the saving music and order comes, there is an obvious parallel with the Christian story of crucifixion, communion and redemption, as well as with other non-Christian stories of the god's sacrifice, communion and salvation. In Rilke's poetry the theme culminates in the Orpheus myth, but there are several earlier instances. At the end of the *Stundenbuch* it is said of St Francis: "da war er ausgeteilt", he was dispersed, distributed. And in "Orpheus. Eurydike. Hermes" we read of Eurydike that she was "ausgeteilt wie hunderfacher Vorrat", distributed like hundredfold provision. In the "Requiem for a Friend", the ghost of the departed, new to death, is for the first time dispersed in the All, "zum ersten Mal im All zerstreut". In his translation Stephen Mitchell understands "zerstreut" in the sense of distracted, translating it as bewildered, but undoubtedly both senses are meant together.[88] This is clear if only from the repetition of the word. What disturbs the poet is that in this new dispersal of death she is still distracted:

> daß du zerstreut,
> zum ersten Mal im All zerstreut ...

In the case of Orpheus it is a god who dies, who is dismembered and distributed. This clearly echoes the Christian Passion story, and it could be said that Rilke is linking up here with another strand in the orphic tradition, namely the frequent mediaeval identification of Orpheus with Christ. Christ is the true Orpheus, *verus Orpheus*, who, as *summus musicus* and *primus cantor*, truly tames and redeems the wilderness of the world. But if there is this echo in Rilke, it is certainly not in the spirit of the mediaeval identification. It might be said that if there is any divinity here, it is nature itself, the sonnet's last word, into which we are absorbed and to which we give voice. Of this divinity, Orpheus, to whose music not only the animals and birds, but the trees and the rocks listened, is, one might say, the proper mediator, as Christ is the mediator in the Christian story. However, one should not push the analogy too far. To read some kind of exclusive nature religion into Rilke is probably to make his poetry more doctrinaire than it really is.

Zweiter Teil

I

Atmen, du unsichtbares Gedicht!
Immerfort um das eigne
Sein rein eingetauschter Weltraum. Gegengewicht,
in dem ich mich rhythmisch ereigne.

Einzige Welle, deren
allmähliches Meer ich bin;
sparsamstes du von allen möglichen Meeren, –
Raumgewinn.

Wieviele von diesen Stellen der Räume waren schon
innen in mir. Manche Winde
sind wie mein Sohn.

Erkennst du mich, Luft, du, voll noch einst meiniger
  Orte?
Du, einmal glatte Rinde,
Rundung und Blatt meiner Worte.

This first of the twenty-nine sonnets of the second part, with its particularly compact and dense imagery, was, in fact, the last of them to be written. The motif of breath is so often metaphorically and symbolically used by Rilke, it would be confusing to attempt to follow all the by-ways of cross-reference. Besides, it seems one should be particularly wary here of speaking of symbols. It is in the first place "real" breathing that is meant. According to Katharina Kippenberg's report, Rilke said of this sonnet that it is to be taken quite literally, without seeking any kind of symbolic meaning.[89] In any case it is clear that what is here meant is not the breath that suggests brevity and what is fleeting, but the rhythmical exchange and intercourse in the life-preserving act of breathing. In that elemental act man does, after all, have contact with that "nowhere without no" the Eighth Elegy speaks of:

> that pure
> unsuperintended element one breathes,
> endlessly knows, and never craves.

In that Elegy, too, the one that speaks of man's destiny of always being opposite, breath signifies the ideal, as in the contrast between protection in the womb or nest with the later homelessness of adult human life: here all is distance; there it was breath: "Hier ist alles Abstand / und dort wars Atem". As the very rhythm of life, breathing is, in the basic metaphor of the sonnet, said to be a poem, and the end of the sonnet may even recall the tall tree in the ear of the opening sonnet, the creative power of music, just as the word "Blatt", leaf, has the double association with nature and the human word. The suggestion in the breathing imagery not only of exchange but of change, relates to the general orphic context of metamorphosis and to that ethical basis of the sonnet cycle: acquiescence in change.

II

> So wie dem Meister manchmal das eilig
> nähere Blatt den *wirklichen* Strich
> abnimmt: so nehmen oft Spiegel das heilig
> einzige Lächeln der Mädchen in sich,
>
> wenn sie den Morgen erproben, allein, –
> oder im Glanze der dienenden Lichter.
> Und in das Atmen der echten Gesichter,
> später, fällt nur ein Widerschein.
>
> *Was* haben Augen einst ins umrußte
> lange Verglühn der Kamine geschaut:
> Blicke des Lebens, für immer verlorne.
>
> Ach, der Erde, wer kennt die Verluste?
> Nur, wer mit dennoch preisendem Laut
> sänge das Herz, das ins Ganze geborne.

The effectiveness of the poem is the vivid imagery of the fleeting, flickering glimpses of beauty, in the firelight, in the lamp-light, in the mirror, sometimes captured for a moment, like by the artist with a hasty master-stroke on the nearest paper to hand, brief glimpses of lost living. The "moral" of the sonnet is in the final tercet. These losses are only known and preserved by whoever sings of the heart that is born "into the whole". The sentiment, the faith in the whole, is the same as in the elegy on the whole which takes and gives account of everything – "im Ganzen ist immer schon alles gezählt" – the elegy to Marina (referred to here later): "O, die Verluste ins All", on the losses into the whole.

III

Spiegel: noch nie hat man wissend beschrieben,
was ihr in euerem Wesen seid.
Ihr, wie mit lauter Löchern von Sieben
erfüllten Zwischenräume der Zeit.

Ihr, noch des leeren Saales Verschwender –,
wenn es dämmert, wie Wälder weit...
Und der Lüster geht wie ein Sechzehn-Ender
durch eure Unbetretbarkeit.

Manchmal seid ihr voll Malerei.
Einige scheinen *in* euch gegangen –,
andere schicktet ihr scheu vorbei.

Aber die Schönste wird bleiben –, bis
drüben in ihre enthaltenen Wangen
eindrang der klare gelöste Narziß.

Rilke often seems to counter transitoriness with spaciousness and in this sonnet the mirrors are defined as spaces of time. They are another world than the world we live in and out of our reach, "unbetretbar". Yet they are also spaces through which we slip into that other world. (The mirror-reflection in the second stanza compares and combines the images of empty hall – ball-room perhaps – and the forest at dusk, of the chandelier and the stag with the sixteen-pointed antler.) The theme is, perhaps, the porousness of life, open to another world. Just as a sieve is really "filled with holes", has holes as its essence, so too our lives are filled with the holes through which we have entry to the other world. Our nature, and *a forteori* the nature of the artist, is self-reflective, narcissistic. In the Narcissus poems of the late period Narcissus is "fated to see himself" – "Ihm aber war gesetzt, daß er sich sähe" – and fated too to lose himself in reflection, to have a weak, yielding kernel, forever in flight:

> Nachgiebige Mitte in mir, Kern voll Schwäche,
> der nicht sein Fruchtfleisch anhält. Flucht, o Flug
> von allen Stellen meiner Oberfläche.[90]

Narcissus is a myth of consuming passion, but the final suggestion here is that in that other world, "drüben", beauty is set free and preserved.

IV

O dieses ist das Tier, das es nicht giebt.
Sie wußtens nicht und habens jeden Falls
– sein Wandeln, seine Haltung, seinen Hals,
bis in des stillen Blickes Licht – geliebt.

Zwar *war* es nicht. Doch weil sie's liebten, ward
ein reines Tier. Sie ließen immer Raum.
Und in dem Raume, klar und ausgespart,
erhob es leicht sein Haupt und brauchte kaum

zu sein. Sie nährten es mit keinem Korn,
nur immer mit der Möglichkeit, es sei.
Und die gab solche Stärke an das Tier,

daß es aus sich ein Stirnhorn trieb. Ein Horn.
Zu einer Jungfrau kam es weiß herbei –
und war im Silber-Spiegel und in ihr.

A sonnet with a striking single image of the unicorn, which is fabulous and yet fed so strongly with the possibility of being that it puts forth a horn. The final reference is as in Malte's reflections on the tapestries of *La Dame à la Licorne* in the Musée de Cluny in Paris, depicting the woman holding up the mirror to show the unicorn its reflected image.[91] The final line suggests that the unicorn, traditionally the image of virginity, is reflected, not only in the mirror, but in the virgin herself. For once Rilke offers an explanation of the sonnet as a celebration, in the image of the mirror, of humanity's dreams and ideals, albeit an explanation in the context of his misgivings about any approach to the *Sonnets* that would seek to analyse and explain, rather than remain open and responsive. This is in a letter to Countess Sizzo, which is important for one's whole approach to the *Sonnets*, suggesting that one should respond as immediately as possible to each poem in its own right, with as little recourse as possible to cross-reference and allusion. Rilke wrote:

> Ich glaube, daß kein Gedicht in den Sonetten an Orpheus etwas meint, was nicht völlig darin ausgeschrieben steht, oft allerdings mit seinen verschwiegensten Namen. Alles was "Anspielung" wäre, widerspricht für meine Überzeugung dem unbeschreiblichen *Da-Sein* des Gedichts. So ist auch im Einhorn keine Christus-Parallele mitgemeint; sondern nur alle Liebe zum Nicht-Erwiesenen, nicht Greifbaren, aller Glaube an den Wert und die Wirklichkeit dessen, was unser Gemüt durch die Jahrhunderte aus sich erschaffen und erhoben hat, mag darin gerühmt sein ... In der Tat, je mehr uns die Tradition äußerlich abgeschränkt und abgeschnürt wird, desto entscheidender wird es für uns *ob* wir fähig bleiben, zu den weitesten und geheimsten Überlieferungen der Menschheit offen und leitend zu bleiben. Die Sonette an Orpheus sind, so verstehe ich sie immer mehr, ein im letztem Gehorsam geleisteter effort in dieser tiefen Richtung ...

Das Einhorn hat alle, im Mittelalter immerfort
gefeierte Bedeutungen der Jungfräulichkeit:
daher ist behauptet, es, das Nicht-Seiende für
den Profanen, sei, sobald es erschiene, in dem
Silberspiegel, den ihm die Jungfrau vorhält
(siehe: Tapisserien des XV. Jahrhunderts) und
"in ihr", als in einem zweiten ebenso reinen,
ebenso heimlichen Spiegel.[92]

V

Blumenmuskel, der der Anemone
Wiesenmorgen nach und nach erschließt,
bis in ihren Schooß das polyphone
Licht der lauten Himmel sich ergießt,

in den stillen Blütenstern gespannter
Muskel des unendlichen Empfangs,
manchmal *so* von Fülle übermannter,
daß der Ruhewink des Untergangs

kaum vermag die weitzurückgeschnellten
Blätterränder dir zurückzugeben:
du, Entschluß und Kraft von *wie*viel Welten!

Wir, Gewaltsamen, wir währen länger.
Aber *wann*, in welchem aller Leben,
sind wir endlich offen und Empfänger?

There could hardly be an image of power more discreet
or delicate – or more typical of Rilke – than the
opening image of the flower-muscle. Flowers and their
manner of existence, usually in contrast to the life of
man, is a frequent theme, as in the Eighth Elegy:

We've never, no, not for a single day
pure space before us, such as that which flowers
endlessly open into.

The theme of the anemone sonnet might be summed up in a line from a later dedicatory poem, the injunction in its last and italicised line that flower-existence be our model: "uns sei Blume-sein groß".[93] Within this general theme, Rilke picks out the anemone in particular. In a poem from 1907, one of the poems under the heading: *Improvisationen aus dem Capreser Winter*, we read of the need to "close over infinity" in the lines:

> Und doch, du weißt, wir können also so
> am Abend zugehn, wie die Anemonen,
> Geschehen eines Tages in sich schließend,
> und etwas größer morgen wieder aufgehn.
> Und so zu tun, ist uns nicht nur erlaubt,
> das ist es, was wir sollen: Zugehn lernen
> über Unendlichem.

How painful this being open to everything is, is suggested in one of those – worthy of Kafka – self-analysing letters of Rilke to Lou. He wrote in June 1914 from Paris:

> Ich bin wie die kleine Anemone, die ich einmal in Rom im Garten gesehen habe, sie war tagsüber so weit aufgegangen, daß sie sich zur Nacht nicht mehr schließen konnte. Es war furchtbar sie zu sehen in der dunklen Wiese, weitoffen, immer noch aufnehmend in den wie rasend aufgerissenen Kelch, mit der vielzuvielen Nacht über sich, die nicht alle wurde. Und daneben alle die klugen Schwestern, jede zugegangen um ihr kleines Maaß Überfluß. Ich bin auch so heillos nach außen gekehrt, darum auch zerstreut von allem, nichts ablehnend, meine Sinne gehn, ohne mich zu fragen, zu allem Störenden über, ist da ein Geräusch, so geb ich mich auf und *bin* dieses Geräusch, und da alles einmal auf Reiz eingestellte, auch gereizt sein will, so will ich im Grunde gestört sein und bins ohne Ende.[94]

The anemone of the sonnet does close, although almost overpowered by fulness, its total receptivity a reproach to man, who is not, not yet, open and receptive.

VI

Rose, du thronende, denen im Altertume
warst du ein Kelch mit einfachem Rand.
Uns aber bist du die volle zahllose Blume,
der unerschöpfliche Gegenstand.

In deinem Reichtum scheinst du wie Kleidung um
    Kleidung
um einen Leib aus nichts als Glanz;
aber dein einzelnes Blatt ist zugleich die Vermeidung
und die Verleugnung jedes Gewands.

Seit Jahrhunderten ruft uns dein Duft
seine süßesten Namen herüber;
plötzlich liegt er wie Ruhm in der Luft.

Dennoch, wir wissen ihn nicht zu nennen, wir raten ...
Und Erinnerung geht zu ihm über,
die wir von rufbaren Stunden erbaten.

In a presentation copy of the *Sonnets* Rilke noted:

Die antike Rose war eine einfache "Eglantine", rot und gelb, in den Farben, die in der Flamme vorkommen. Sie blüht hier, im Wallis, in einzelnen Gärten.[95]

The sonnet celebrates the history of the rose, to Rilke the supreme flower and, up to the final epitaph, the image of completeness – "Rose, toi, ô chose par excellence complète",[96] but a completeness that, as he emphasised in a letter to Countess Gneisenau, includes all the nuances of wilting and fading, which we must come to accept:

... Denn das Welken und Welksein und Sich-daran-Hingeben ist eine Schönheit mehr neben der Schönheit dessen, was kommt und treibt und trägt... [97]

The rose is inextricably bound up with our lives and the sonnet celebrates the inexhaustible significance, the innumerable meanings and memories it has accumulated for us over the centuries. Leishman remarks with justice regarding this sonnet:

> The development, through the ages, of the rose, and of its meaning in and for us, was the kind of "progress" that most interested Rilke.

VII

Blumen, ihr schließlich den ordnenden Händen
    verwandte,
(Händen der Mädchen von einst und jetzt),
die auf dem Gartentisch oft von Kante zu Kante

wartend des Wassers, das sie noch einmal erhole
aus dem begonnenen Tod –, und nun
wieder erhobene zwischen die strömenden Pole
fühlender Finger, die wohlzutun

mehr noch vermögen, als ihr ahnet, ihr leichten,
wenn ihr euch wiederfandet im Krug,
langsam erkühlend und Warmes der Mädchen, wie
    Beichten,

von euch gebend, wie trübe ermüdende Sünden,
die das Gepflücktsein beging, als Bezug
wieder zu ihnen, die sich euch blühend verbünden.

The theme of the poem, the relationship between plant life and human life, is given in the opening line and the final tercet has that key-word of Rilke's relationship creed "Bezug". The cohesion and unity are reflected in the run-on lines and the one-sentence structure. There may be something too precious or too obtrusive in the clichés of decadence, the warm and weary sins of the confessional, the monotonously repetitive vowel-music: "erkühlend, trübe, ermüdend, Gepflücktsein, blühend, verbünden", but its sentiment of relating to a wholeness of life and death, flowering and fading, is central to Rilke.

VIII

Wenige ihr, der einstigen Kindheit Gespielen
in den zerstreuten Gärten der Stadt:
wie wir uns fanden und uns zögernd gefielen
und, wie das Lamm mit dem redenden Blatt,

sprachen als Schweigende. Wenn wir uns einmal
    freuten,
keinem gehörte es. Wessen wars?
und wie zergings unter allen den gehenden Leuten
und im Bangen des langen Jahrs.

Wagen umrollten uns fremd, vorübergezogen,
Häuser umstanden uns stark, aber unwahr, – und
    keines
kannte uns je. *Was* war wirklich im All?

Nichts. Nur die Bälle. Ihre herrlichen Bogen.
Auch nicht die Kinder ... Aber manchmal trat eines,
ach ein vergehendes, unter den fallenden Ball.

                (In memoriam Egon von Rilke)

Egon von Rilke, who died in childhood, was the youngest child of Rilke's uncle Jaroslav, and remained, he said in a letter to his mother in 1924, one of his most unforgettable memories:

> Ich denke oft an ihn und komme immer wieder auf seine Figur zurück, die mir unbeschreiblich ergreifend geblieben ist. Viel "Kindheit", das Traurige und Hilflose des Kindseins, verkörpert sich mir in seiner Gestalt, in der Halskrause, die er trug, dem Hälschen, dem Kinn, den schönen und durch das Schielen entstellten braunen Augen. So rief ich ihn im Anschluß an jenes VIII. Sonett, das die Vergänglichkeit ausdrückt, noch einmal hervor, nachdem er ja schon in den "Aufzeichnungen des M. L. Brigge" seinerzeit als Vorbild für den kleinen Erik Brahe, den als Kind Verstorbenen, gedient hatte.[98]

According to this letter, therefore, the sonnet expresses transitoriness and in the very evocative and effective imagery of the poem, its sense of the shadowy and insubstantial, the only abiding reality is the rising and falling rhythm of the ball. The ball is one of Rilke's most persistent symbols. According to Schmidt-Pauli he referred to his poem "Der Ball", one of the *New Poems*, as his best. She writes in her reminiscences:

> Da blieb Rilke stehen und zeigte auf einen Baum, der allein mitten auf dem beschnittenen Rasen stand: "Sehen Sie – das ist es, was ich will und nichts anderes: ich möchte diesen Baum so sagen, daß nur noch den Baum in meinen Worten spräche, so wie er ist, ohne irgend etwas von Rilke hinzuzufügen. Mein Gedicht "Der Ball" ist mir in dieser Weise ganz gelungen. Da habe ich gar nichts als das fast Unaussprechbare einer reinen Bewegung ausgesprochen – und darum ist es mein bestes Gedicht".[99]

(That poem begins with the same sense of union, through the transfer of warmth, as in the sonnet just considered, on the cut flowers.[100])

The falling ball of this Eighth Sonnet is an image, not only of transitoriness in childhood, but paradoxically also of permanence in an "everywhere", of enrichment in reciprocity, as in one of Rilke's latest poems, in the last poem for Erika Mitterer, with the image of the "dared" ball, thrown out of our "no-where" into the over-arching "over-all".[101]

On the 31st January 1922, two days before the onset of the *Sonnets* Rilke had written the poem "Solang du Selbstgeworfenes fängst, ist alles", in which again the ball symbolises, as the only abiding reality, an eternal interplay, to which, it seems, one must surrender oneself as the rest of nature does. It is not enough to catch what we ourselves have thrown. Only when one suddenly becomes the catcher of the ball that an eternal partner has thrown with masterly flourish, in one of those arches out of God's great bridge-building, only then is catching a true capacity, capacity of a whole world. And if one has even the strength and courage to throw it back, or, more wonderfully, forgets strength and courage and has already thrown (as the year throws the birds, the migrating swarms, cast across the oceans from an older to a younger warmth) only in such a venture is one's participating play a valid one:

> Solang du Selbstgeworfnes fängst, ist alles
> Geschicklichkeit und läßlicher Gewinn –;
> erst wenn du plötzlich Fänger wirst des Balles,
> den eine ewige Mitspielerin
> dir zuwarf, deiner Mitte, in genau
> gekonntem Schwung, in einem jener Bögen
> aus Gottes großem Brücken-Bau:
> erst dann ist Fangen-Können ein Vermögen, –
> nicht deines, einer Welt. Und wenn du gar
> zurückzuwerfen Kraft und Mut besäßest,
> nein, wunderbarer: Mut und Kraft vergäßest
> und schon geworfen *hättest* ... (wie das Jahr
> die Vögel wirft, die Wandervogelschwärme,
> die eine ältre einer jungen Wärme
> hinüberschleudert über Meere –) erst
> in diesem Wagnis spielst du gültig mit.[102]

IX

Rühmt euch, ihr Richtenden, nicht der entbehrlichen
    Folter
und daß das Eisen nicht länger an Hälsen sperrt.
Keins ist gesteigert, kein Herz – , weil ein gewollter
Krampf der Milde euch zarter verzerrt.

Was es durch Zeiten bekam, das schenkt das Schafott
wieder zurück, wie Kinder ihr Spielzeug vom vorig
alten Geburtstag. Ins reine, ins hohe, ins thorig
offene Herz träte er anders, der Gott

wirklicher Milde. Er käme gewaltig und griffe
strahlender um sich, wie Göttliche sind.
Mehr als ein Wind für die großen gesicherten Schiffe.

Weniger nicht, als die heimliche leise Gewahrung,
die uns im Innern schweigend gewinnt
wie ein still spielendes Kind aus unendlicher Paarung.

Although this sonnet is one of those Rilke copied out to send to Lou as being the sonnets that appeared to him to be the best,[103] it seems at first unrelated to the orphic world. Like the next sonnet it is concerned with modernity and expresses Rilke's notorious scepticism about progress, about the vaunted advance in humanitarianism. It is an accusation directed at a world that thinks it has become more merciful, having laid aside, as dispensable, older instruments of torture. But the heart has not changed, has not become the great open gate through which the god of mercy could come, majestic, powerful, yet childlike. As always Rilke is distrustful of outward show; true metanoia is inward. This attitude leads, not without reason, to the accusation that Rilke is apolitical and unhistorical. It is not at all that Rilke ignores the horrors of reality, to which he is as acutely sensitive as Malte, who reflects on the terrible existence and persistence of all the terrors of gallows, torture-chambers, madhouses:

> alles das ist von einer zähen Unvergänglichkeit, alles
> das besteht auf sich und hängt, eifersüchtig auf
> alles Seiende, an seiner schrecklichen Wirk-
> lichkeit.[104]

The problem is not the ignoring of evil, but the manner in which Rilke appears to absolve it. Rejecting the false claims of humanitarian progress, just as he rejects the consolations of a religion that would put everything right in the end, he puts his trust rather in an all-embracing orphic myth that cancels contradictions, insisting that the human heart, if it is open enough, can indeed comprehend and celebrate the whole of existence, darkness and death, no less than light and life. This is the burden, for example, of that long, uncompromising letter to Countess Sizzo, rejecting any consolation other than that recourse to wholeness.[105]

X

Alles Erworbne bedroht die Maschine, solange
sie sich erdreistet, im Geist, statt im Gehorchen, zu sein.
Daß nicht der herrlichen Hand schöneres Zögern mehr
 prange,
zu dem entschlossenern Bau schneidet sie steifer den
 Stein.

Nirgends bleibt sie zurück, daß wir ihr *ein* Mal
 entrönnen
und sie in stiller Fabrik ölend sich selber gehört.
Sie ist das Leben, – sie meint es am besten zu können,
die mit dem gleichen Entschluß ordnet und schafft und
 zerstört.

Aber noch ist uns das Dasein verzaubert; an hundert
Stellen ist es noch Ursprung. Ein Spielen von reinen
Kräften, die keiner berührt, der nicht kniet und
 bewundert.

Worte gehen noch zart am Unsäglichen aus ...
Und die Musik, immer neu, aus den bebendsten Steinen,
baut im unbrauchbaren Raum ihr vergöttlichtes Haus.

Again Rilke's scepticism about and reaction against a secularised, technological and desanctified modernity. It is in two parts, at first deploring the hubris of the soulless machine, but then finding that life is still divinely magical, mysterious, musical, only to be approached in an attitude of admiration, of adoration. The strangest word is perhaps the "unbrauchbar" of the last line. What he extols is the non-utilitarian, and music, which in the dedication poem "Musik" is said to be "from every wherefore freed", "von jeglichem Wozu befreit",[106] provides at the end the fine contrasting image to the utilitarian and technological. Music builds a house of vibrating stones, unusable and yet infinitely hospitable and inhabitable.

XI

Manche, des Todes, entstand ruhig geordnete Regel,
weiterbezwingender Mensch, seit du im Jagen beharrst;
mehr doch als Falle und Netz, weiß ich dich, Streifen von Segel,
den man hinuntergehängt in den höhligen Karst.

Leise ließ man dich ein, als wärst du ein Zeichen,
Frieden zu feiern. Doch dann: rang dich am Rande der Knecht,
– und, aus den Höhlen, die Nacht warf eine Handvoll von bleichen
taumelnden Tauben ins Licht ...
Aber auch *das* ist im Recht.

Fern von dem Schauenden sei jeglicher Hauch des Bedauerns,
nicht nur vom Jäger allein, der, was sich zeitig erweist,
wachsam und handelnd vollzieht.

Töten ist eine Gestalt unseres wandernden Trauerns ...
Rein ist im heiteren Geist,
was an uns selber geschieht.

It is doubtless in the case of this sonnet that many readers will find it most difficult to follow what Leishman calls "the remorseless logic of Rilke's religion". It is a poem on hunting and the underlying image is explained by Rilke himself:

> Bezugnehmend auf die Art, wie man, nach altem Jagdgebrauch, in gewissen Gegenden des Karsts, die eigentümlich bleichen Grotten-Tauben, durch vorsichtig in ihre Höhlen eingehängte Tücher, indem man diese plötzlich auf eine besondere Weise schwenkt, aus ihren unterirdischen Aufenthalten scheucht, um sie, bei ihrem erschreckten Ausflug, zu erlegen.[107]

Leishman finds the italicised declaration repugnant to reason and humanity, asking if one could say at the site of an extermination camp:

> Far from the gazer remain every emotion but gladness,
> not from the Nazis alone ...?

To this one may object that Rilke is speaking of hunting, not of the Holocaust. All the same the emphatic affirmation of killing's rightness is a hard saying, though consistent with the all-embracing orphic affirmation and paralleled by many similar references in Rilke. Magda von Hattingberg recalls her conversation with Rilke in which, to her astonishment, he defended hunting. The end of that conversation expresses Rilke's mistrust of any merely humane and so partial judgement, allowing only an impartial standpoint of totality:

> "Aber schließlich: was wissen wir!" schloß er seufzend, "reicht denn nicht im Grunde alles über uns hinaus, über unser Innigstes und Geringstes, hat nicht denn alles um uns in der Welt Gesetz und Geltung auch *ohne* uns?"

Later in her reminiscences Benvenuta relates the Indian legend Rilke told her "in answer as it were to so many unresolved questions of human existence". The legend told of three old monks, who were so holy that when they bathed their cloaks they hung miraculously in the air. One day as they bathed they watched an eagle snatching a fish from the water. The first monk said: "Bad eagle!", and his cloak fell to the ground. The second monk said: "Poor fish!" and his cloak fell to the ground. The third monk watched in silence as the eagle disappeared in the distance and his cloak remainded hanging in the air.[108]

The poem "Vollmacht" calls on us to join the company of hunters, who are "always in the right", in urgent contact with life; because they are so living, the infinitely affirmed animal approaches the fatal blow:

> Diese sind ewig im Recht: dringend dem Leben Genahte;
> weil sie Lebendige sind, tritt das unendlich bejahte
> Tier in den tödlichen Schlag.[109]

One may be sceptical about this concept of the animal that is thus endlessly affirmed, but Rilke is uncompromisingly consistent in this allegiance to the totality of existence. This is documented in letters at all stages of his life. To Ilse Erdmann he wrote in 1916:

> Unsere Sicherheit muß irgendwie ein Verhältnis zum Ganzen werden, zu einer Vollzähligkeit; Sichersein heißt für uns die Unschuld des Unrechts gewahren und die Gestalthaftigkeit des Leidens zugeben; heißt Namen ablehnen, um dahinter die einzigen Bildungen und Verbindungen des Schicksals, wie Gäste, zu ehrwürdigen ... heißt nichts verdächtigen, hinausdrängen ... Die Unsicherheit ganz groß nehmen –: in einer unendlichen Welt wird auch die Sicherheit unendlich ... [110]

In 1901 he had written to Clara's brother:

> Es geht eine große und ewige Schönheit durch die ganze Welt, und diese ist gerecht über den kleinen und den großen Dingen verstreut; denn es gibt im Wichtigen und Wesentlichen keine Ungerechtigkeit auf der ganzen Erde.[111]

It is the burden of his advice in his many counselling letters. To Kappus he wrote:

> Und im übrigen lassen Sie sich das Leben geschehen. Glauben Sie mir: das Leben hat recht, auf alle Fälle.[112]

And in the so-called *Workman's Letter* of 1922 he writes:

> Man sollte sich anstrengen in jeder Macht, die ein Recht über uns beansprucht, gleich alle Macht zu sehen, die ganze Macht, Macht überhaupt, die Macht Gottes. Man sollte sich sagen, es gibt nur *eine*, und die geringe, die falsche, die fehlerhafte so verstehen, als wär sie das, was uns mit Recht ergreift. Würde sie nicht unschädlich auf diese Weise? Wenn man in jeder Macht, auch in arger und boshafter, immer die Macht selbst sähe, ich meine das, was zuletzt recht behält, mächtig zu sein, überstünde man da nicht, heil sozusagen, auch das Unberechtigte und Willkürliche?[113]

Significantly he speaks there of the ever-justified power of God and it is in this theological context that Rilke's creed is perhaps most understandable, namely understood as a reaction against what he found to be the restrictive and constricting creed of his Catholic upbringing. Rilke's orphic myth with its unbounded affirmation is in direct opposition to the Christian myth of original sin and its deadly consequences and of that redemption in which the crooked shall be made straight. Rilke's God is the "God of Totality", as in that most notorious of Rilke's letters, the "anti-socialist" letter to Hermann Pongs in 1924, in which he so passionately rejects the concept of a corrected world. The poet, he declares there:

> müßte nichts mehr fürchten und ablehnen als eine korrigierte Welt, darin die Zwerge gestreckt sind und die Bettler bereichert. Der Gott der Vollzähligkeit sorgt dafür, daß diese Varietäten

> nicht aufhören, und es wäre die oberflächlichste Einstellung, wollte man die Freude des Dichters an dieser leidenden Vielfalt für eine ästhetische Ausrede halten.[114]

There could hardly be a more remorseless, to use Leishman's word, rejection both of any secular socialism and of the Christian tradition of a corrected world, as expressed, for example, in the so-called "Golden Sequence", the *Veni, Sancte Spiritus*:

> Lava quod est sordidum,
> Riga quod est aridum,
> Sana quod est saucium.
> Flecte quod est rigidum,
> Fove quod est frigidum,
> Rege quod est devium.

Not only does he oppose the Christian creed, he is equally opposed to a humanistic moral criticism of nature as exemplified in Thomas Mann's monk-narrator with his "Fie upon Nature and her indifference", "Ein Pfui der Natur und ihrem Gleichmut".[115] "The Whole" is appealed to by Rilke again and again. A letter to Countess Dietrichstein in 1919 may serve as a final example. It might seem unexceptionable when he says that man should not appeal to the cruelty in nature to excuse his own, but in the end he is subscribing to a totality that includes darkness, evil, death, no less than light, goodness, life:

> Wenn der Mensch doch aufhörte, sich auf die Grausamkeit in der Natur zu berufen, um seine eigene zu entschuldigen! Er vergißt, wie unendlich schuldlos auch noch das Fürchterlichste in der Natur geschieht, sie sieht ihm nicht zu, sie hat keine Distanz dazu, – sie ist im Ensetzlichsten ganz, auch ihre Fruchtbarkeit ist darin, ihre Großmut –; es [ist], wenn man so sagen soll, auch nichts anderes als ein Ausdruck ihrer Fülle. Ihr Bewußtsein besteht in ihrer Vollzähligkeit, weil sie alles enthält, enthält sie auch das Grausame, – der Mensch aber, der nie imstand sein wird, alles zu umfassen, ist nie sicher,

wo er das Furchtbare wählt, sagen wir den Mord –, auch schon das Gegenteil dieses Abgrundes zu enthalten, und so richtet ihn im selben Augenblick seine Wahl, da sie ihn zu einer Ausnahme macht, zu einem vereinzelten, vereinseitigten Wesen, welches ans Ganze nicht mehr angeschlossen ist. Der gute, der rein entschlossene, der fähige Mensch würde das Böse, das Verhängnis, das Leid, das Unheil, den Tod nicht aus den gegenseitigen Verhältnissen ausschließen können, aber wo ihn eines davon träfe oder er zur Ursache dessen würde, da stünde er nicht anders da als ein Heimgesuchter in der Natur, oder heimsuchend wider seinen Willen, wäre er wie der verheerende Bach, der anschwillt durch irgendwelche herabstürzenden Tauwässer, deren Einmündung in ihn er sich nicht zu verschließen vermag.[116]

XII

Wolle die Wandlung. O sei für die Flamme begeistert,
drin sich ein Ding dir entzieht, das mit Verwandlungen
    prunkt;
jener entwerfende Geist, welcher das Irdische
    meistert,
liebt in dem Schwung der Figur nichts wie den
    wendenden Punkt.

Was sich ins Bleiben verschließt, schon *ists* das
    Erstarrte;
wähnt es sich sicher im Schutz des unscheinbaren
    Grau's?
Warte, ein Härtestes warnt aus der Ferne das Harte.
Wehe –: abwesender Hammer holt aus!

Wer sich als Quelle ergießt, den erkennt die Erkennung;
und sie führt ihn entzückt durch das heiter Geschaffne,
das mit Anfang oft schließt und mit Ende beginnt.

Jeder glückliche Raum ist Kind oder Enkel von
    Trennung,
den sie staunend durchgehn. Und die verwandelte
    Daphne
will, seit sie lorbeern fühlt, daß du dich wandelst in
    Wind.

The theme of the sonnet is immediately stated: Will change; that nothing remains and that all constantly changes is to be affirmed. Looking at the sequence of images, it may be that the four stanzas refer in turn to the four elements of classical antiquity, fire, earth, water and air. The first stanza suggests that if things constantly seem to withdraw from us, as if consumed by flame, this is to be welcomed, for in all this movement nothing is more in accordance with the spirit behind earthly existence than the turning point. The turning point is perhaps that point of balance between loss, in so far as the individual is conceived of in isolation, and gain, in so far as the individual is seen in relation to the whole. The element of earth may be suggested in the second stanza as apparently the most solid – but to seek to remain the same is a kind of rigidity that is devoid of life, a hardness that will be destroyed by that same spirit that masters the earth. The element of water in the third stanza suggests by contrast the person who lives in accordance with the law of flux and who is accepted into that harmonious creation, which in its changefulness has neither beginning nor end. The last stanza, repeating the admonition to recognise the necessity of parting, to be like the air, ever moving and all pervading, finally recalls the myth of Daphne, who was turned into a laurel-tree. Probably one should not see any more precise reference to details of the Daphne myth. Daphne simply represents metamorphosis and a return to or union with the totality of nature.

One notes that this laurel existence is imagined as feeling, willing, thinking in some fashion. Is this nothing more than a pathetic fallacy? Questions like that remain unanswered. The only certainty is change. In the draft of a poem on the words of the Lord to John on Patmos, God says: "Sieh ich dulde nicht daß einer bleibe", "See, I do not suffer that any should remain".[117] In the First Elegy we read:

Denn Bleiben ist nirgends
For staying is nowhere.

Yet it is probably significant that in a copy of the *Duino Elegies* for Carossa, Rilke wrote dedicatory lines on the lasting kingdom of transformation, "das bleibende Reich der Verwandlung", suggesting permanence in some other sense, in some other context. In his interpretation, Mörchen is very cautious about using terms for change like transformation or transsubstantiation or metamorphosis, any term that might, he would feel, too comfortingly imply some kind of survival of an essence behind all the impermanence of appearances.[118] He prefers to emphasise in Rilke an acquiescence in the fact and the finality of death. It is doubtful, however, if Rilke has that kind of definitiveness.

XIII

Sei allem Abschied voran, als wäre er hinter
dir, wie der Winter, der eben geht.
Denn unter Wintern ist einer so endlos Winter,
daß, überwinternd, dein Herz überhaupt übersteht.

Sei immer tot in Eurydike –, singender steige,
preisender steige zurück in den reinen Bezug.
Hier, unter Schwindenden, sei, im Reiche der Neige,
sei ein klingendes Glas, das sich im Klang schon
    zerschlug.

Sei – und wisse zugleich des Nicht-Seins Bedingung,
den unendlichen Grund deiner innigen Schwingung,
daß du sie völlig vollziehst dieses einzige Mal.

Zu dem gebrauchten sowohl, wie zum dumpfen und
    stummen
Vorrat der vollen Natur, den unsäglichen Summen,
zähle dich jubelnd hinzu und vernichte die Zahl.

This sonnet, too, begins by announcing its admonitory theme: anticipate all farewells, or more literally, be ahead of all leave-taking. To the mother of the girl to whom he dedicated the sonnets, Rilke wrote just after their composition:

> Heute schicke ich Ihnen nur *ein* Sonett mit, weil es mir, im ganzen Zusammenhang, das naheste ist und, am Ende, das überhaupt gültigste...[119]

He wrote some days later in similar terms to Katharina Kippenberg. The thirteenth sonnet of the second part is for him the most valid of all, he says:

> Es enthält alle übrigen und es spricht das aus, was, ob es mich gleich noch weit übertrifft, eines Tages meine reinste endgültigste Erreichung, mitten im Leben, müßte sein dürfen.[120]

If the Eighth Elegy depicts man as always in the attitude of someone who is departing and ends with the line: "we live our lives, for ever taking leave", the *Sonnets*, in their more positive manner, call for an affirmation, even an anticipation of all leave-taking, including the ultimate wintriness, the endless winter of death. In this sonnet the Orpheus-Eurydike story is, exceptionally, directly referred to. If the Orpheus of myth would seem to be the appropriate mentor for knowledge of the underworld, whether he is so appropriate for the affirmation of death in Rilke's sense is another matter. The Orpheus of these sonnets is not only a very different Orpheus to the impatient and undiscerning Orpheus of "Orpheus. Eurydike. Hermes", he is probably very different also to the Orpheus of the classical stories. For Orpheus here, or the person addressed in the poem, who follows in the footsteps of Orpheus, climbs back from the underworld in a spirit of praise, enriched by the knowledge of death, which is accepted into life. The starkest admonition is probably the line: "Sei – und wisse zugleich des Nicht-Seins Bedingung". Be – and know at the same time non-being's condition. The syntax is difficult. The genitive of non-being probably does not mean "the condition of non-being", but rather "non-being as the condition of the possibility of being". It is a line that can give rise to much speculative interpretation, with recourse particularly to Heidegger. But it is probably truer to the spirit of Rilke's poetry to concentrate on the idea that death should be brought back from the distance to which it has been banished. As often with such themes, it is easier to approach it from the negative side; to understand what Rilke is protesting against is easier than to understand what he proposes. In a letter of 1915, which is largely theological and in which he suggests that God is, as it were, a never explored region of the human spirit, for too long excluded and seen as being outside, he goes on to say: and the same happened with death. So that it would not interrupt us in our search for the meaning of life, it was held at bay, banished, regarded as life's contradiction, the adversary lying in wait and ready to pounce, whereas any meaningful affirmation of life, Rilke would seem to imply, must be affirmation of a totality that includes death.[121]

The phrase: "this one single time" recalls the emphatic "once" of the ninth elegy:

> Just *once*,
> everything, only for *once*. *Once* and no more. And we, too,
> once. And never again. But this
> having been *once, though only once,*
> having been *once* on earth – can it ever be cancelled?

And the "Schwingung" or vibration of the preceding line recalls the vibration of "venturing earliest music" at the end of the First Elegy with its myth of the birth of music out of the spirit of tragedy, – one could say perhaps like the ringing of the shattering glass in the preceding lines. The final lines are an admonition once more to experience oneself as absorbed in a totality that is beyond number and that sets our divisive reckoning at naught. Incidentally, Mörchen, determined to exclude from Rilke anything that he would regard as false comfort, here pushes his line of reasoning to its limits. According to him the final "Zahl" or number means the sum-total, which too must be destroyed, in the case of which the condition of non-being must also be accepted. But this is a very unlikely interpretation, involving a very uncharacteristic use of the term "Zahl", which in Rilke – part of his anti-rationalistic prejudice – has the negative associations of small-minded numbering, isolating, dividing. "Zahl" certainly does not mean sum-total here. Rather is Holthusen right when he says:

> Was ist "Zahl", wenn nicht ein Prinzip der Vereinzelung und damit der Vielfalt und der Unterscheidung! Dadurch daß ich mich (hinzu-) zähle, vernichte ich die Zahl ...[122]

Rilke ends the sonnet, as he often does, with the conviction of abundance or superabundance in the totality of existence, what he calls here "Vorrat der vollen Natur", full nature's stock. Recalling the winter image of this sonnet, the poem "Winterliche Stanzen" has as its theme "Natur ist göttlich voll", nature is divinely full and for this fulness "Vorrat", stock, store, supply, is a favourite term, not only in his poetry. The horrors of the times, he says in a letter towards the end of the war, cannot diminish his faith in vouching "für die wunderbaren Vorräte des Lebens", for life's marvellous store.[123]

Throughout the *Sonnets* one is aware of the urgently and decisively personal sense in which the mythology is meant. With regard to the "most valid" sonnet, this is brought out by a letter to Nanny Wunderly-Volkart, in which he speaks of his meetings with Angela Guttmann, who was gravely ill, and of the anguish of their threatened separation. Yet they had somehow been able to perceive "the whole", rather that the "alas so fleeting moment", the "appointment to meet in the heavens", the "bond through God that is the greatest freedom from person to person". One evening they had anticipated, *known* their parting, put their parting, so to speak, behind them:

> Aber ein Maaß ist da, ein größeres Maaß unserer so merkwürdigen Zugehörigkeit, – daraus entstand die Milderung, daß nicht mehr der Moment, der, ach, so verlierbare! ins Auge gefaßt wurde, sondern das Ganze, die Verabredung im Gestirn, die Bindung durch Gott, die ja die größte Freiheit ist von Mensch zu Mensch ... Eines Abends legten wir den Abschied gewissermaßen schon hinter uns, *wußten* ihn.[124]

XIV

Siehe die Blumen, diese dem Irdischen treuen,
denen wir Schicksal vom Rande des Schicksals leihn,
aber wer weiß es! Wenn sie ihr Welken bereuen,
ist es an uns, ihre Reue zu sein.

Alles will schweben. Da gehn wir umher wie Beschwerer,
legen auf alles uns selbst, vom Gewichte entzückt;
o was sind wir den Dingen für zehrende Lehrer,
weil ihnen ewige Kindheit glückt.

Nähme sie einer ins innige Schlafen und schliefe
tief mit den Dingen –; o wie käme er leicht,
anders zum anderen Tag, aus der gemeinsamen Tiefe.

Oder er bliebe vielleicht; und sie blühten und priesen
ihn, den Bekehrten, der nun den Ihrigen gleicht,
allen den stillen Geschwistern im Winde der Wiesen.

One of many poems in which Rilke contrasts human existence, with its sense of destiny, its ballast of doubt and distraction that has man in thrall, with the free-flowing life, "unbeschwert", of the flower, faithful to the earth and the natural processes of growth and decay. It is we who are disruptive, as in the next sonnet, imposing our weight of consciousness on the rest of creation. In the poem "Vor Weihnachten 1914" it is said of things that "the heaviness of our limbs, what there is of leave-taking in us, comes over them":

> Die Schwere unsrer Glieder
> was an uns Abschied ist, kommt über sie.[125]

And the theme of this sonnet is anticipated in "Ode an Bellman", where it is said that "we, whatever we become, have weight, we are not the floating ones":

> denn,
> Bellman, wir sind ja nicht die Schwebenden.
> Was wir auch werden, hat Gewicht.[126]

The sonnet is one of the most smoothly-flowing ones, as a correlative to that light, eternally child-like "natural" life. If only, the sonnet concludes, man too could be in communion with the rest of creation, converted to the purely affirmative form of existence. One could object that this is an inhuman ideal and that indeed the ideal of eternal childhood is itself unnatural. Similarly one could suggest that it is the *Elegies* rather than the *Sonnets* which give a positive purpose and a sense of service to human destiny, which is here merely ballast and an imposition. But to see any inconsistency in this would be to make inappropriately all-inclusive demands of any one poem. Both attitudes are present in Rilke, but this sonnet is concerned, rather than with humanity's contribution, with what man, the all too interfering teacher, can learn from the rest of nature.

XV

O Brunnen-Mund, du gebender, du Mund,
der unerschöpflich Eines, Reines, spricht, –
du, vor des Wassers fließendem Gesicht,
marmorne Maske. Und im Hintergrund

der Aquädukte Herkunft. Weither an
Gräbern vorbei, vom Hang des Apennins
tragen sie dir dein Sagen zu, das dann
am schwarzen Altern deines Kinns

vorüberfällt in das Gefäß davor.
Dies ist das schlafend hingelegte Ohr,
das Marmorohr, in das du immer sprichst.

Ein Ohr der Erde. Nur mit sich allein
redet sie also. Schiebt ein Krug sich ein,
so scheint es ihr, daß du sie unterbrichst.

A sonnet essentially on the same theme as the preceding one, the fulfillment and wholeness of the earth, with which the human element merely seems to interfere, as the jug interrupts the self-communing flow of the fountain, at once speaking mouth and listening ear. As always in these sonnets, this image of natural life includes death and the dead, as the water comes "past the graves" from the faraway mountains. If the introduction of the human at the end comes as an interruption, there is at the same time, implicit in the imagery – for the fountain is the work of human hands – the suggestion that man, too, can be in harmony with the earth. Leishman suggests that "the stone mouth of the fountain is a symbol for the poet's mouth, through which, also, earth is only talking to herself". This may be to over-interpret, but it is true that Rilke constantly celebrates those creations of man he feels to be in harmony with natural life. He had a particular fondness for such artifacts as the Roman fountains and, in that mission that he imagines for man in the *Elegies*, it is especially those human creations that must be internalised and immortalised:

> Are we, perhaps, here just for saying: House,
> Bridge, Fountain, Gate, Jug, Fruit tree, Window ...

XVI

> Immer wieder von uns aufgerissen,
> ist der Gott die Stelle, welche heilt.
> Wir sind Scharfe, denn wir wollen wissen,
> aber er ist heiter und verteilt.
>
> Selbst die reine, die geweihte Spende
> nimmt er anders nicht in seine Welt,
> als indem er sich dem freien Ende
> unbewegt entgegenstellt.
>
> Nur der Tote trinkt
> aus der hier von uns *gehörten* Quelle,
> wenn der Gott ihm schweigend winkt, dem Toten.
>
> *Uns* wird nur das Lärmen angeboten.
> Und das Lamm erbittet seine Schelle
> aus dem stilleren Instinkt.

This is another of those eleven sonnets Rilke copies out for Lou as being those he considered the best. E. M. Butler, on the other hand, clearly finding the sonnet to be a prime example of Rilke's "orphic nonsense", declares in her acerbic fashion that the sestet is "a lapse into pure inanity".[127] Certainly the sonnet is one of the most disputed. Mörchen says it is one of the most difficult, giving rise to much very speculative interpretation. He gives as an example the interpretation of the "free end" in the second stanza by both Angelloz and Kretschmar as "Freitod", suicide.[128]

One might also note Leishman's fanciful speculation on the same phrase:

> We may imagine the offering as being extended towards the god on the end of a long pole, like the collecting-box used in some churches, at home and abroad: the "free end" (das freie Ende) will then be the end nearest to the god, the end we are not holding.

Regarding the final lines, which he does "not yet fully understand", Leishman more persuasively recalls a conversation he had in the Black Forest with a village priest:

> ... and he told me that every sheep and lamb, cow and calf, had its own particular bell, and would often refuse to go out to pasture until this bell had been duly fastened to its neck.

With reference to the unmoved or silent response of the god, Mörchen himself notes, as always, important cross-references. He reminds us that Rilke underlined the passage in Psalm 50 beginning:

> Ich will von deinem Hause Stiere nicht nehmen noch Böcke aus deinen Ställen. Denn alles Wild im Walde ist mein ...

and noted himself in the margin: "Gott nimmt nichts an". And Mörchen reminds us of the reference in the French poems to man's advance to a silent god:

> Si l'on chante un dieu,
> ce dieu vous rend son silence.
> Nul de nous ne s'avance
> que vers un dieu silencieux.[129]

More doubtful is Mörchen's own equation of the god of this sonnet with death.

There are, therefore, many difficulties in detail and one has only to compare the different translations to see how conflicting understandings can be. Yet the overall sense and structure of this sonnet seem clear enough. It is constructed around the contrast between, on the one hand, the orphic world of the god and of nature itself with its quieter instinct, a world that is serene and silent, omnipresent and dispersed in a healing wholeness – the image of the god that is "aufgerissen" and "verteilt" may be a reference to the manner of Orpheus' death, but more importantly it echoes the dispersal in death of St. Francis in the *Stundenbuch* – and on the other hand the world of man with his "need to know", disruptive and divisive, sharp-edged and noisy. Man has cut himself off from the ultimate source, which he now only distantly hears. Again Rilke's mistrust of humanity's knowingness, which is a fall from grace, albeit given a purpose in the "mission" of the *Elegies*.

XVII

Wo, in welchen immer selig bewässerten Gärten, an, welchen
Bäumen, aus welchen zärtlich entblätterten Blüten-Kelchen
reifen die fremdartigen Früchte der Tröstung? Diese
köstlichen, deren du eine vielleicht in der zertretenen Wiese

deiner Armut findest. Von einem zum anderen Male
wunderst du dich über die Größe der Frucht,
über ihr Heilsein, über die Sanftheit der Schale,
und daß sie der Leichtsinn des Vogels dir nicht
                vorwegnahm und nicht die Eifersucht

unten des Wurms. Giebt es denn Bäume, von Engeln beflogen,
und von verborgenen langsamen Gärtnern so seltsam gezogen,
daß sie uns tragen, ohne uns zu gehören?

> Haben wir niemals vermocht, wir Schatten und
>   Schemen,
> durch unser voreilig reifes und wieder welkes
>   Benehmen
> jener gelassenen Sommer Gleichmut zu stören?

This is one of many "nevertheless" poems of Rilke, as is, more obviously, the twenty-second sonnet below: "O trotz Schicksal: die herrlichen Überflüsse". As if in response to the preceding sonnets with their theme of human impatience and disruptiveness, this sonnet, one of the most smoothly-running in rhythm and single-minded in imagery, celebrates the fact that, in spite of an apparently shallow and shadowy existence, we ever and again experience the wholeness and redemption of the hidden angelic world we have not after all destroyed and are nourished by its fruits. This is the true consolation as opposed to the false consolations Rilke so often and so passionately rejects, as in that bitter description of the garish "fairground of consolation" in the Tenth Elegy. He rejects in particular the consolations of Christianity, which, as he said in a diary entry of 1900, he found himself unable to believe in.[130]

The Church should have recognised the essential "inconsolability", "Trostlosigkeit" of existence, he writes to Pastor Zimmermann in 1921.[131]

So he rings the changes on that theme summed up in the letter to Countess Sizzo in the phrase: "aller Trost ist trübe". On the other hand he had written to Princess Marie in 1915 on the urgent need for "Tröstungen", but adding that these we must find in ourselves:

> ... es müßte nur unser Auge eine Spur schauender, unser Ohr empfangender sein, der Geschmack einer Frucht müßte uns vollständiger eingehen, wir müßten mehr Geruch

> aushalten, und im Berühren und Angerührtsein
> geistesgegenwärtiger und weniger vergeßlich sein
> –: um sofort aus unseren nächsten Erfahrungen
> Tröstungen aufzunehmen, die überzeugender,
> überwiegender, wahrer wären als alles Leid, das
> uns je erschüttern kann.[132]

The kind of comfort he rejects is that which devalues the earthly, but otherwise he treasures the consolations we find in that to which we are most accustomed, in wind, in fire:

> Aber sonst sei dir die Tröstung teuer,
> die du im Gewohntesten erkennst.
> Wind ist Trost, und Tröstung ist das Feuer.[133]

Indeed Rilke refers, in one of his dedications, to the sonnet cycle itself as a "closed circle of joy and consolation", a "geschlossenen Umkreis der Freude und Tröstung".[134]

XVIII

> Tänzerin: o du Verlegung
> alles Vergehens in Gang: wie brachtest du's dar.
> Und der Wirbel am Schluß, dieser Baum aus Bewegung,
> nahm er nicht ganz im Besitz das erschwungene Jahr?
>
> Blühte nicht, daß ihn dein Schwingen von vorhin
>   umschwärme,
> plötzlich sein Wipfel von Stille? Und über ihr,
> war sie nicht Sonne, war sie nicht Sommer, die Wärme,
> diese unzählige Wärme aus dir?
>
> Aber er trug auch, er trug, dein Baum der Ekstase.
> Sind sie nicht seine ruhigen Früchte: der Krug,
> reifend gestreift, und die gereiftere Vase?
>
> Und in den Bildern: ist nicht die Zeichnung geblieben,
> die deiner Braue dunkler Zug
> rasch an die Wandung der eigenen Wendung
>   geschrieben?

As in the case of any other sonnet, one can look for explanations outside the context of the poem itself or indeed of Rilke's work generally. Some would see here the influence of Valery and his dialogue *L'âme et la danse*, which Rilke had translated shortly before.[135] But while parallels can be noted, they do not seem significantly to alter or add to our understanding of the sonnet and it is perhaps better to keep in mind that advice of Rilke to Countess Sizzo that, in order to understand the sonnets, she should keep to "what is written there" and avoid "allusions". In the context of the whole work the sonnet can be read as a tribute to Wera, the young dancer to whose memory the cycle is dedicated, but beyond that it is a tribute to the art of the dance and through that to all art, the movement of the dancer being associated here with the turning of the potter's wheel and the "fruit" of the potter's art, the jug and the vase, and the lines swiftly drawn in the air by the dark eyebrows of the dancer describing as it were a wall-painting. But the art of the dance has particular significance as the art-form that most approprately represents Rilke's "art-religion". Central to this sonnet, as to the whole cycle, is the idea of mutability, of transitoriness and mortality, and the mutability is most evident in dance, though inherent, in Rilke's understanding, in all art forms. Rilke's belief in art is not in any sense in art as something static, defying the flux of life. It is rather the transmutation of mutability and the theme of the sonnet is summed up in the opening definition of dance as the transference, transmutation of mutability into movement. There is no sense in Rilke that art and nature are opposed, rather do they coincide. The "ecstasy" of art does not take us out of nature, but rather out of ourselves into nature, is a "tree of ecstasy". As in the opening sonnet, what the orphic art produces is said to be a tree, with the emphasis here on the fact that it is a tree made out of the movement of mutability, a tree that is fruitful and with all the warmth of animation.

XIX

Irgendwo wohnt das Gold in der verwöhnenden Bank
und mit Tausenden tut es vertraulich. Doch jener
Blinde, der Bettler, ist selbst dem kupfernen Zehner
wie ein verlorener Ort, wie das staubige Eck unterm
  Schrank.

In den Geschäften entlang ist das Geld wie zuhause
und verkleidet sich scheinbar in Seide, Nelken und Pelz.
Er, der Schweigende, steht in der Atempause
alles des wach oder schlafend atmenden Gelds.

O wie mag sie sich schließen bei Nacht, diese immer
  offene Hand.
Morgen holt sie das Schicksal wieder, und täglich
hält es sie hin: hell, elend, unendlich zerstörbar.

Daß doch einer, ein Schauender, endlich ihren langen
  Bestand
staunend begriffe und rühmte. Nur dem Aufsingenden
  säglich.
Nur dem Göttlichen hörbar.

This is one of those sonnets that is not so much difficult to understand as difficult in the uncompromising demands made on the reader by Rilke's creed. For Stahl is surely right that a glorification, a "beatification" of poverty, "Seligsprechung der Armut" is the subject of the poem, continuing the tradition of that notorious line in the *Stundenbuch* "Denn Armut ist ein großer Glanz aus Innen".[136] It is true that the poem is also, and very satirically and graphically, a castigation of capitalist greed, though this is hardly likely to mollify hostile critics, who will be equally cynical about this sweeping condemnation of the obscenities of banks and businesses by the fastidious and well-protected poet. To be sure, one can say that the dictum "Denn Armut ist ein großer Glanz aus Innen" is not only much reviled but also much maligned, for poverty in the over-all context of the *Stundenbuch* has a more mystical meaning, is an attribute of all who would approach the God of the *Stundenbuch* and *par excellence* of the God Himself. The maligned line introduces the litany on God's poverty beginning "Du bist der Arme, du der Mittellose ...", akin to the total selflessness or self-emptying, in death as in life, of St. Francis. But it would be shirking the issue not to recognise that Rilke also means "real" poverty and the plight of the destitute. One has to recall again that letter to Pongs, its God of Totality and its fear of a corrected world. Much of the long letter is like a gloss on this sonnet. Rilke writes:

> Die Lage eines Menschen ändern, bessern wollen, heißt, ihm für Schwierigkeiten, in denen er geübt und erfahren ist, andere Schwierigkeiten anbieten, die ihn vielleicht noch ratloser finden. Wenn ich irgendwann die imaginären Stimmen des Zwerges oder des Bettlers in der Form meines Herzens ausgießen konnte, so war das Metall dieses Gusses nicht aus dem Wunsche gewonnen, der Zwerg oder der Bettler möchten es weniger schwer haben; im Gegenteil, nur durch eine Rühmung ihres unvergleichlichen Schicksals vermochte der zu ihnen plötzlich entschlossene Dichter wahr und gründlich zu sein, und er müßte nichts mehr fürchten und ablehnen als eine korrigierte Welt, darin die Zwerge gestreckt sind und die Bettler bereichert. Der Gott der Vollzähligkeit sorgt dafür, daß diese Varietäten nicht aufhören, und es wäre die oberflächlichste Einstellung, wollte man die Freude des Dichters an dieser leidenden Vielfalt für eine ästhetische Ausrede halten ... In einer Welt, die das Göttliche in eine Art Anonymität aufzulösen versucht, mußte jene humanitäre Überschätzung platzgreifen, die von der menschlichen Hülfe erwartet, was sie nicht geben kann. Und göttliche Güte ist so

> unbeschreiblich an göttliche Härte gebunden,
> daß eine Zeit, die jene, der Vorsehung vorweg,
> auszuteilen unternimmt zugleich auch die
> ältesten Vorräte der Grausamkeit unter die
> Menschen reißt. (Wir habens erlebt.)[137]

As well as balking at its apparent lack of humanity, one may question the logic, especially as Rilke himself so often seems to "dissolve divinity in anonymity". But so far as the poetry is concerned it is less the logic than the emotional force that matters. Rilke's rejection of a corrected world, his horror of interference is rooted in very personal experience, going back to his childhood. One thinks of the poem "Dauer der Kindheit" which recalls the child's afternoons, alone at home, faced in the mirrors with the riddle of himself, until the "others" return and overcome him – they drown out, frustrate all that things had begun to entrust to him, it all becomes "theirs" again:

> Nachmittage, da es allein blieb, von einem
>   Spiegel zum andern
> starrend; anfragend beim Rätsel des eigenen
> Namens: Wer? Wer? – Aber die Andern
> kehren nachhause und überwältigens,
> Was ihm das Fenster, was ihm der Weg,
> was ihm der dumpfe Geruch einer Lade
> gestern vertraut hat: sie übertönens, vereitelns.
> Wieder wird es ein Ihriges.[138]

This is one of the most persistent and heartfelt themes, the interference that falsifies, as in the programmatic lines of the *Stundenbuch* with their refusal to "bend", for to be bent is to be betrayed:

> Nirgends will ich gebogen bleiben,
> denn dort bin ich gelogen, wo ich gebogen bin[139]

This in turn leads to that uncompromising praise of things as they are, including the "deadly" and the "monstrous". That praise is central to Rilke's creed and is his "way of withstanding":

> Oh, sage, Dichter, was du tust?
> – Ich rühme.
> Aber das Tödliche und Ungetüme,
> wie hältst du's aus, wie nimmst du's hin?
> – Ich rühme.[140]

It is central in particular to the myth of the orphic poet as in the sixth sonnet "Rühmen, das ists! Ein zum Rühmen Bestellter ..." On the one hand this centrality of praise might seem unexceptionable and in the tradition of Christian praise of creation, but it is as uncompromisingly opposed to Christian comforts as to the exaggerated humanitarian expectations he refers to in the Pongs letter. The sonnet culminates in the celebration of the persistence and the "perpetually open hand" of the beggar, something that one can only "understand with astonishment", that indeed is apprehensible only to a god or the god-like singer.

XX

Zwischen den Sternen, wie weit; und doch, um wievieles
    noch weiter,
was man am Hiesigen lernt.
Einer, zum Beispiel, ein Kind ... und ein Nächster, ein
    Zweiter –,
o wie unfaßlich entfernt.

Schicksal, es mißt uns vielleicht mit des Seienden
    Spanne,
daß es uns fremd erscheint;
denk, wieviel Spannen allein vom Mädchen zum Manne,
wenn es ihn meidet und meint.

Alles is weit –, und nirgends schließt sich der Kreis.
Sieh in der Schüssel, auf heiter bereitetem Tische,
seltsam der Fische Gesicht.

Fische sind stumm ..., meinte man einmal. Wer weiß?
Aber ist nicht am Ende ein Ort, wo man das, was der
    Fische
Sprache wäre, *ohne* sie spricht?

This sonnet might at first seem out of place within the orphic cycle. Leisi says that the poem is remote from the central ideas of the orphic circle and so difficult to interpret in that context.[141] Its theme, however, is quite central to Rilke's deepest concerns. That theme is: the sense of "astronomical" distances, as it were out of hearing and beyond communication, between all things, between us and the world, between our selves – as in the Seventh Elegy: "Denn auch das Nächste ist weit für die Menschen" – and the hope – as in the Fifth Elegy: "Engel: es wäre ein Platz, den wir nicht wissen ..." – that somewhere, at the limits of language, there is a place of silent communicabilty and communion. The idea of distance, especially the distance between people, most of all where they are closest, recurs throughout Rilke's writings, most often in the early years. It is expressed, for example, by the eponymous hero of the early story *Der Totengräber*.[142] Around the same time, in 1901, Rilke writes in a letter:

> Ein *Miteinander* zweier Menschen ist eine Unmöglichkeit und, wo es doch vorhanden scheint, eine Beschränkung, eine gegenseitige Übereinkunft, welche einen Teil oder beide Teile ihrer vollsten Freiheit und Entwicklung beraubt. Aber, das Bewußtsein vorausgesetzt, daß auch zwischen den nächsten Menschen unendliche Fernen bestehen bleiben, kann ihnen ein wundervolles Nebeneinanderwohnen erwachsen, wenn es ihnen gelingt, die Weite zwischen sich zu lieben, die ihnen die Möglichkeit gibt, einander immer in ganzer Gestalt und vor einem großen Himmel zu sehen![143]

It is impossible to ignore the special pleading in this and so many similar sentiments, not least in his letters to his wife, particularly in those early years – though it remains a constant concern – when he is so obsessed with the need to establish the first condition of his creative life, the condition of solitude.

But that personal concern aside, the sense of distance is central to Rilke's thinking, not only distance from the world and from one another, but distance from our own destiny, indeed distance is that destiny. The lines here:

> Schicksal, es mißt uns vielleicht mit des
>   Seienden Spanne,
> daß es uns fremd erscheint,

echo the lines from the *New Poems*:

> Fremd, wie niebeschrieben
> sieht mich mein Schicksal an.[144]

Soon after the composition of the *Sonnets* Rilke wrote to Lotti von Wedel:

> Ein denkendes, ein uns mitwissendes Schicksal ... ja, oft wünschte man durch ein solches bestärkt und bestätigt zu sein; aber wärs nicht zugleich

> sofort ein uns von außen anschauendes, ein uns zuschauendes mit dem wir nicht mehr allein wären? Daß wir einem "blinden Schicksal" eingelegt sind, ihm innewohnen, ist doch gewissermaßen die Bedingung unseres eigenen Blicks, unserer schauenden Unschuld. – Erst durch die "Blindheit" unseres Schicksals sind wir mit dem wunderbar Dumpfen der Welt, das heißt mit dem Ganzen, Unübersehlichen und uns Übertreffenden recht tief verwandt ...[145]

The culminating idea here is, as it is again and again in Rilke, the idea of the "relationship" to the "whole". Rilke's rejection of any Christian or quasi-Christian belief is very deep-rooted, but equally insistent is the "theology of totality" that he puts in its place. Ever and again he puts his trust in union, communion, communication with the totality of existence. At the same time there is always the suggestion that this is extraordinarily difficult to achieve, an almost impossible demand on the potentials of language, as indeed the total affirmation that the God of Totality demands is extraordinarily difficult. This is expressed at the end of the sonnet with the strange – "seltsam" – image of the fish and fish language. (There is an ambiguity in the final line, in that "sie" could refer to fish or to language. This probably does not materially alter the sense, but the more likely reference is to language.) The ultimate communication, communion, is at a depth of language akin to silence. To Frau Wunderly Rilke had written about the "innermost language" he is striving to attain, striving to reach ever deeper levels and only able to sense "how one might speak there, where there is silence":

> ... aber man gelangt nur um eine minimale Schicht hinab, man bleibt im Ahnen, wie sich dort reden ließe, wo das Schweigen ist.[146]

There is no doubt that with the *Elegies* and *Sonnets* Rilke felt he had somehow reached into that innermost language or silence. One of the many dedicatory verses he wrote in the following years invokes the deeper, more inward silence that touches the roots of speech:

> Schweigen. Wer inniger schwieg,
> rührt an die Wurzeln der Rede.[147]

The next day he wrote the dedicatory verses for Robert and Jenny Faesi:

> Wo sich langsam aus dem Schon-Vergessen
> einst Erfahrnes uns entgegenhebt,
> rein gemeistert, milde, unermessen
> und im Unantastbaren erlebt:
>
> Dort beginnt das Wort, wie wir es meinen;
> seine Geltung übertrifft uns still.
> Denn der Geist, der uns vereinsamt, will
> völlig sicher sein, uns zu vereinen.[148]

A few weeks later he writes the dedicatory verses for Hulewicz, his Polish translator, expressing his conviction that, behind all language and independent of our endeavour to build the bridges of relationship, there is an inexpressible communality that communicates itself to us:

> Glücklich, die wissen, daß hinter allen
> Sprachen das Unsägliche steht;
> daß, von dort her, ins Wohlgefallen
> Größe zu uns übergeht!
>
> Unabhängig von diesen Brücken
> die wir mit Verschiedenem baun:
> so daß wir immer, aus jedem Entzücken
> in ein heiter Gemeinsames schaun.[149]

XXI

Singe die Gärten, mein Herz, die du nicht kennst; wie in
 Glas
eingegossene Gärten, klar, unerreichbar.
Wasser und Rosen von Ispahan oder Schiras,
singe sie selig, preise sie, keinem vergleichbar.

Zeige, mein Herz, daß du sie niemals entbehrst.
Daß sie dich meinen, ihre reifenden Feigen.
Daß du mit ihren, zwischen den blühenden Zweigen
wie zum Gesicht gesteigerten Lüften verkehrst.

Meide den Irrtum, daß es Entbehrungen gebe
für den geschehnen Entschluß, diesen: zu sein!
Seidener Faden, kamst du hinein ins Gewebe.

Welchem der Bilder du auch im Innern geeint bist
(sei es selbst ein Moment aus dem Leben der Pein),
fühl, daß der ganze, der rühmliche Teppich gemeint ist.

Little needs to be explained in this poem. Ispahan and Shiras were two ancient Iranian provincial capitals, Ispahan famous for its well-watered fruitful landscape and Shiras for its flower-gardens. The theme of the poem is the abundance and superabundance of life, of the totality of which, even where it is most remote and out of reach, we all partake. Rilke wrote several more sonnets at the same time, which he did not include in the sequence. One of them is very similar – not included perhaps precisely because it is a variation on the same theme – with the line: We are the heirs, nevertheless, of those sung gardens, going on to elaborate on that idea: we are heirs to the gardens, fountains, villas, to the gods of the past, to the beliefs of the past. But the abundance must be earned by the receptive attitude and the sonnet here is admonitory with a sequence of imperatives, sing, show, know, feel, to the heart, which must first make that decision – the same decision to be open as in the anemone poem – which he refers to in one of his letters as a decision for the earth, "sich zur Erde entschließen",[150] and which is given poetic expression in the Ninth Elegy: "Erde, du liebe, ich will". Of course one feels yet again that identifying and isolating the idea of the poem is really saying very little about it, about the musicality, which may be what matters most.

XXII

O trotz Schicksal: die herrlichen Überflüsse
unseres Daseins, in Parken übergeschäumt, –
oder als steinerne Männer neben die Schlüsse
hoher Portale, unter Balkone gebäumt!

O die eherne Glocke, die ihre Keule
täglich wider den stumpfen Alltag hebt.
Oder die *eine*, in Karnak, die Säule,
die fast ewige Tempel überlebt.

Heute stürzen die Überschüsse, dieselben,
nur noch als Eile vorbei, aus dem waagrechten gelben
Tag in die blendend mit Licht übertriebene Nacht.

Aber das Rasen zergeht und läßt keine Spuren.
Kurven des Flugs durch die Luft und die, die sie fuhren,
keine vielleicht ist umsonst. Doch nur wie gedacht.

The many "nevertheless celebration" poems could be said to culminate in this sonnet, celebrating the superabundance of earthly existence, as evidenced by the great objects of the past, the splendid parks, the statues, the sonorous bells. He had once and for a lifetime experienced Easter, he wrote to Lou, when he heard Ivan Welikij, the great bell at Moscow, strike in the darkness.

> Mir war ein einziges Mal Ostern ... als der Ivan Welikij mich schlug in der Dunkelheit, Schlag für Schlag. Das war mein Ostern, und ich glaube es reicht für ein ganzes Leben aus.[151]

He writes in the same terms about the column of the temple at Karnak in the poem "In Karnak wars":

> ... Und jetzt, für unser ganzes Leben,
> die Säule –: jene! War es nicht genug?[152]

At the time of that Egyptian journey he had written to Clara:

> ... diese unbegreifliche Tempelwelt von Karnak, die ich gleich den ersten Abend und gestern wieder im eben erst abnehmenden Monde sah, sah, sah, – mein Gott, man nimmt sich zusammen, sieht mit allem Glaubenwollen beider eingestellten Augen – und doch beginnts über ihnen, reicht überall über sie fort (nur ein Gott kann ein solches Sehfeld bestellen) – da steht eine Kelchsäule, einzeln, eine überlebende, und man umfaßt sie nicht, so steht sie einem über das Leben hinaus, nur mit der Nacht zusammen erfaßt mans irgendwie ...[153]

Contrasted with all of this is the different superabundance of our technological and restlessly rushing age of the aeroplane and artificial light, which leaves no such traces, though that present-day abundance, too, is perhaps not in vain and has lasting value, inwardly if not visibly. The puzzling phrase at the end: "Doch nur wie gedacht" is doubtless to be read in the sense that the Seventh Elegy speaks of the dwindling outwardness of modern life. There is, of course, much that is negative in Rilke's attitude to modernity, something that is more polemically expressed in the Hulewicz letter, where he contrasts modern, "American", empty pseudo-things with the things of our grandparents, infinite storehouses of their humanity.[154] (Professor Butler refers to Rilke's "invincible ignorance" about America and says of that Hulewicz remark:

> This denial of spiritual life to a whole continent, this almost insane assumption that the rhythm of nature, the deep organic connection between life and death – the central theme of the sonnets – did not hold good in the New World reveals Rilke as having attained the very nadir of bombastic nonsense.[155]

Elisabeth Butler's biography is a healthy antidote to any over-credulous reading of Rilke, but this gloss on a rather common-place remark is surely absurd.) In the sonnet the negative attitude is particularly obvious in the image of the exaggerated night-light. It reminds one of a passage from one of his letters from Venice in 1912 when, with his prejudice towards mere tourists, he wrote to the Princess:

> Eigentlich möcht ich gern viel zuhause sein, die Fremden sind doch über Hand und, wehe, wenn man abends über den Marcusplatz kommt und sie alle angeleuchtet findet von den Glühlampen der Illuminierung; dieser stupide Superlativ von Licht vertreibt die letzten Züge aus ihren Gesichtern, sie sehen alle Ah-Ah-Ah aus, ohne Unterschied oder Abstufung; ich weiß nicht wie es kommt, daß sie sich in diesem Zustand untereinander unterscheiden: vermittels des Kellners wahrscheinlich, bei dem sie sitzen.[156]

With those sort of associations the sestet of the sonnet can be read almost altogether negatively, as it is, for example, by Geering, who says that these products of modernity are "bereft of all creativity".[157] It seems more likely, however, that the sonnet is a celebration of life's superabundance, past and present, even if the celebration of the past is more enthusiastic and that of the present more muted, not to say fastidious.

The "glorious superabundance" is invoked "in spite of destiny". Since there are over a hundred references to "Schicksal" in Rilke's poetry, as well as many more in his letters and elsewhere, interpretations by way of cross-reference can lead in many different directions, with the danger of leading too far away from the sonnet. One can note however, as is almost invariably remarked upon, that the word has generally negative connotations in Rilke. At the same time it is, I think, misleading when Leisi says: "Schicksal, ein oft gebrauchtes Wort, bedeutet beim späten Rilke ein Orpheus feindliches Prinzip" and again: "In den Sonetten erscheint das Schicksal immer als Orpheus-Gegner".[158] Rilke himself suggests the definition at one time:

> Ich nenne Schicksal alle äußeren Ereignisse (Krankheiten zum Beispiel einbegriffen), die unvermeidlich eintreten können, eine Geistesdisposition und Erziehung, einsam durch ihre Natur, zu unterbrechen und zu vernichten.[159]

Sickness was indeed to be the last and most terrible test of his celebratory poetry. But that definition of "Schicksal" is in the more particular and personal sense in which he is mainly concerned, as he so often was, with the protection of his own isolation and integrity against outside interference. The more general and fundamental meaning is destiny as presented in the *Elegies* –

> Dieses heißt Schicksal: gegenüber sein
> und nichts als das und immer gegenüber

– with the question why, to what purpose:

> warum dann
> Menschliches müssen – und, Schicksal vermeidend,
> sich sehnen nach Schicksal?

If destiny has negative connotations, it is not because it is "Orpheus-Gegner", but because it is so difficult for man to follow Orpheus:

> Ein Gott vermags. Wie aber, sag mir, soll
> ein Mann ihm folgen durch die schmale Leier?

In spite of the difficulty of this distance-destiny life is "gloriously abundant". If this is the sentiment of the sonnet, it is also the faith by which he lived and died. The main witness to the long-drawn-out agony that led to his death was Frau Wunderly-Volkart, whom he begged to help him to "die his own death" and to whom he also said: "Vergessen Sie nie, Liebe, das Leben ist eine Herrlichkeit!"[160]

XXIII

Rufe mich zu jener deiner Stunden,
die dir unaufhörlich widersteht:
flehend nah wie das Gesicht von Hunden,
aber immer wieder weggedreht,

wenn du meinst, sie endlich zu erfassen.
So Entzognes ist am meisten dein.
Wir sind frei. Wir wurden dort entlassen,
wo wir meinten, erst begrüßt zu sein.

Bang verlangen wir nach einem Halte,
wir zu Jungen manchmal für das Alte
und zu alt für das, was niemals war.

Wir, gerecht nur, wo wir dennoch preisen,
weil wir, ach, der Ast sind und das Eisen
und das Süße reifender Gefahr.

According to Rilke's note this sonnet is addressed "to the reader". This seems to give the sonnet special significance, as if it is particularly prescriptive, encapsulating the meaning and the message of the cycle. At those moments when we are most unsure of ourselves, feel most unprotected, rejected and alone, the poet suggests that it is then we are most ourselves and have come into our own. The very paradoxical creed: "So Entzognes ist am meisten dein", is central to Rilke's ideas and ideals of being free from interference, exposed to a totality that provides no kind of shelter, at home only in this state of being-in-danger. This idea and ideal of danger is something one can see develop throughout Rilke's life and work, as he seems not merely to acknowledge, but to welcome the fact that the old certainties are gone and that the only security must be found in surrender to a totality that has none of the partiality and protectiveness of the religion he was brought up in. "Die Gefahr ist sicherer geworden als die Sicherheit", we read in *Malte*.[161] And in a poem from that Paris period, anticipating later references to the God of totality, he invokes a God, who, unlike the "light" God of childhood – Ach in der Kindheit, Gott: wie warst du leicht" – is now a God, who is "our danger", for only so can he be a God of completeness:

> Herr, sei nicht gut: sei herrlich; widerleg
> das Hörensagen, das sie an dir rühmen:
> zerbrich das Haus, zerstör den Steg
> und wälz ein Nest von Ungetümen
> dem Flüchtling an den Nebenweg.
>
> Denn so sind wir verkauft an kleine Nöte,
> daß alle meinen Jahr um Jahr
> wenn einer ihnen beide Hände böte
> so wär ein Gott. Du Notnacht voller Röte,
> du Feuerschein, du Krieg, du Hunger: töte:
> denn du bist unsere Gefahr.
>
> Erst wenn wir wieder unsern Untergang
> in dich verlegen, nicht nur die Bewahrung,
> wird alles dein sein: Einsamkeit und Paarung,
> die Niederlage und der Überschwang.
> Damit entstehe, was du endlich stillst,
> mußt du uns überfallen und zerfetzen;
> denn nichts vermag so völlig zu verletzen
> wie du uns brauchst, wenn du uns retten willst.[162]

In the uncompleted elegy on childhood "Laß dir, daß Kindheit war ..." the idea is developed that in childhood, too, protection was only a pretence:

> Nicht, daß sie harmlos sei; der behübschende Irrtum,
> der sie verschürzt und berüscht, hat nur vergänglich
>   getäuscht.
> Nicht ist sie sicherer als wir, und niemals geschonter
> keiner der Göttlichen wiegt ihr Gewicht auf. Schutzlos
> ist sie wie wir, wie Tiere im Winter, schutzlos.
> Schutzloser: denn sie erkennt die Verstecke nicht.
>   Schutzlos
> so als wäre sie selber das Drohende. Schutzlos
> wie ein Brand, wie ein Ries', wie ein Gift, wie was umgeht
> nachts im verdächtigen Haus, bei verriegelter Tür.
>
> Denn wer begriffe nicht, daß die Hände der Hütung
> lügen, die schützenden –, selber gefährdet ...

The only true security is in the womb of the earth-mother, in whom we "nevertheless" trust:

>   ... dennoch!
> Was du da nennst, das *ist*
> die Gefahr, die ganze
> reine Gefährdung der Welt –, und so schlägt sie in Schutz um,
> wie du sie rührend erfühlst. Das innige Kindsein
> steht wie die Mitte in ihr, sie *aus*-fürchtend, furchtlos.[163]

Danger is our nature, being the nature of Nature:

> I am danger, else I would not be nature
>
> Ich bin Gefahr, sonst wär ich nicht Natur

he writes in one of the poems for Erika Mitterer, whom he addresses as:

dared child, nowhere secure but in danger:

Gewagtes Kind, nun bist Du nirgends sicher
als in Gefahr.[164]

How the ideal of danger arose out of reaction against the feeling of interfering protectiveness in childhood is brought out particularly clearly in the poem he wrote for Erika Mitterer, "Dauer der Kindheit" referred to already in the context of the Nineteenth Sonnet, with its recall of the child's solitary afternoons, frustrated by the return of the "others". "Possessive love" "betrays" the child to a future that is not his own. His true future, for good or ill, is utterly remote from that "creature under surveillance":[165]

... Liebe umkreist, die besitzende,
das immer heimlich verratene Kind
und verspricht es der Zukunft; nicht seiner.

...

Oh wie weit ists von diesem
überwachten Geschöpf zu allem, was einmal
sein Wunder sein wird, oder sein Untergang.

There is something obsessive in this horror of supervision, "Überwachung". In that letter to Lotti von Wedel, referred to above in the context of the Twentieth Sonnet, a blind fate is preferred and in the Eight Elegy a totally open world of nature, free of human desires and fears, is idealised:

das Reine,
Unüberwachte, das man atmet und
unendlich *weiß* und nicht begehrt ...

That Elegy extols "das freie Tier" and the Seventh Elegy celebrates the beloved:

atmend,
atmend nach seligem Lauf, auf nichts zu, ins Freie.

The celebration of a blessed love that is directed "towards nothing" is central to much that Rilke readers have always found diffcult, those ideas of "Liebe ohne Gegenliebe", of prayer that is "sans but" – "Prié –: vers qui?", he wrote to Mimi Romanelli from Paris:

> La prière est un rayonnement de notre être soudainement incendié, c'est une direction infinie et sans but ...[166]

– of a God, who, as Malte said, is a direction of love, not an object of love from whom a responding love might be feared:

> ... aber konnte ihr wahrhaftiges Herz sich darüber täuschen, daß Gott nur eine Richtung der Liebe ist, kein Liebes-Gegenstand? Wußte sie nicht, daß keine Gegenliebe von ihm zu fürchten war?[167]

That the reaction against protectedness is itself an almost obsessive self-protectiveness is obvious, as in that plea for freedom in the requiem for Paula Modersohn-Becker, in the passage quoted earlier ending:

> Wir haben, wo wir lieben, ja nur dies:
> einander lassen; denn daß wir uns halten,
> das fällt uns leicht und ist nicht erst zu lernen.[168]

The strange danger-ideal of unprotectednss and undirectedness is most easily understood as reaction against the stifling childhood experience. In an early poem "Ich war ein Kind und träumte viel", undated but probably written in 1898, the song of the wandering minstrel: "O Mutter, laß mich frei" is said to be his, the poet's, song and suffering, fate and fortune, his life – "mein Glück", "mein Schicksal", "mein Lied", "mein Leid", "mein Leben".[169] Given his Catholic upbringing, it is not least a struggle for freedom in the sexual sphere and one can similarly read the notorious *Seven Poems* as reaction against childhood repression, with their worship of a "free God" – "der freie Gott" –, a phallic godhead. Here the familiar tree and even "Innenraum" images become graphically, almost grotesquely, sexual – but then it is a Rilke characteristic to edge to the limits of language and imagery:

> Du hast mir, Sommer, der du plötzlich bist,
> zum jähen Baum den Samen aufgezogen.
> (Innen Geräumige, fühl in dir den Bogen
> der Nacht, in der er mündig ist.)
> Nun hob er sich und wächst zum Firmament,
> ein Spiegelbild das neben Bäumen steht.
> O stürz ihn, daß er, umgedreht
> in deinen Schooß, den Gegen-Himmel kennt,
> in den er wirklich bäumt und wirklich ragt.
> Gewagte Landschaft, wie sie Seherinnen
> in Kugeln schauen. Jenes Innen
> in das das Draußensein der Sterne jagt.[170]

From the childhood experience of protection and providence as repression and limitation Rilke creates the ideal of total exposure, of danger and freedom, of all-embracing affirmation. Often this ideal seems to be an inhuman one and indeed both *Elegies* and *Sonnets* acknowledge a distinct human destiny, which cannot be like the animal of the Eight Elegy "free from death", and find a purpose for that destiny in the recreation of creation in humanity's "inner space". So he writes in one of the late Muzot poems:

> Durch den sich Vögel werfen, ist nicht der
> vertraute Raum, der die Gestalt dir steigert.
> (Im Freien, dorten, bist du dir verweigert
> und schwindest weiter ohne Wiederkehr.)
>
> Raum greift aus uns und übersetzt die Dinge:
> daß dir das Dasein eines Baums gelinge,
> wirf Innenraum um ihn, aus jenem Raum,
> der in dir west. Umgieb ihn mit Verhaltung.
> Er grenzt sich nicht. Erst in der Eingestaltung
> in dein Verzichten wird er wirklich Baum.[171]

But the ideal remains one of totally exposed openness. The sonnet acknowledges that, although we have outgrown youthful illusions and can no longer be satisfied with old certainties, we still hanker after support – "Bang verlangen wir nach einem Halt" – but if we feel that things withdraw from us, as it were dismiss us, we should celebrate this as our freedom, our emulation of and union with the rest of creation. A fragment from the Paris years anticipates this theme of a world that, astonishingly, does not seek security or foothold, but throws itself into freedom:

> Staune, siehe, wie keines
> Boden verlangt und verläßlichen Haltes.
> Ins Freie wirft sich die Welt.[172]

Whatever one may think of this "religion" of unprotected exposure and total affirmation, Rilke practised it with astonishing consistency up to the harrowing end. In the last weeks he wrote to Frau Wunderly:

> Très Chère, jour et nuit, jour et nuit: l'Enfer! on l'aura connu! Merci que de tout votre être (je le sens) vous m'accompagnez dans ces régions anonymes. Le plus grave, le plus long: c'est d'abdiquer: devenir "le malade". Le chien malade est encore chien, toujours. Nous à partir d'un certain degré de souffrances insensées, sommes-nous encore nous? Il faut devenir le malade, apprendre ce métier absurde sous l'oeil des médecins.[173]

The last fragmentary poem "Komm du, du letzter, den ich anerkenne", with the lines:

> Ganz rein, ganz planlos frei von Zukunft stieg
> ich auf des Leidens wirren Scheiterhaufen.[174]

is his last and most painful affirmation. This final "total freedom" is "totally pure". "Rein" is probably the most significant epithet in Rilke's vocabulary. As the word in its various forms occurs over two hundred times in the poetry, the associations are countless. From the period of the *Elegies* and *Sonnets* and after, typical examples of the use of the epithet would be those written in February 1922 in this poem:

> Mehr nicht sollst du wissen als die Stele
> und im reinen Stein das milde Bild:
> beinah heiter, nur so leicht als fehle
> ihr die Mühe, die auf Erden gilt.
>
> Mehr nicht sollst du fühlen als die reine
> Richtung im unendlichen Entzug ...[175]

or in 1924 in the poem "Shawl":

> ... So eingewirkt in schmiegender Figur
> ins leichte Wesen dieser Ziegenwolle,
> ganz pure Glück, unbrauchbar von Natur
> rein aufgegeben an das wundervolle
>
> Geweb in das das Leben überging.
> O wieviel Regung rettet sich ins reine
> Bestehn und Überstehn von einem Ding.[176]

But most relevant to the sonnet and the concept of pure danger –

> die ganze
> reine Gefährdung der Welt

– is the use of the epithet in the *Elegies* and *Sonnets*, in particular the image of pure, unsupervised space in the Eighth Elegy:

> *Wir* haben nie, nicht einen einzigen Tag,
> den reinen Raum vor uns, in den die Blumen
> unendlich aufgehn. Immer ist es Welt
> und niemals Nirgends ohne Nicht: das Reine,
> Unüberwachte, das man atmet und
> unendlich *weiß* und nicht begehrt.

In the *Sonnets* themselves the epithet is used many times, from the opening image: "Da stieg ein Baum. O reine Übersteigung!", to what is perhaps its most significant context in the "most valid" sonnet, with its injunction to follow Orpheus and establish that "pure relation" with totality, with the "full store of nature" that includes the realm of death:

> Sei immer tot in Eurydike –, singender steige,
> preisender steige zurück in den reinen Bezug.

Rilke's poetry is inseparable from his life and in life, too, he followed the ideal of freedom, of total exposure, with single-minded determination. In his *Testament* the first condition was the exclusion of any ecclesiastical support:

> Sollte ich in eine schwere Krankheit fallen, die am Ende auch den Geist verstört, so bitte, ja beschwöre ich meine Freunde, jeden priesterlichen Beistand, der sich andrängen könnte, von mir fernzuhalten. Schlimm genug, daß ich, in den körperlichen Nöthen meiner Natur, den Vermittler und Verhandler, im Arzte, zulassen mußte; der Bewegung meiner Seele, aufs Offene zu, wäre jeder geistliche Zwischenhändler kränkend und zuwider.[177]

And in his last days he said to Frau Wunderly: "Verhelfen Sie mir zu *meinem* Tod, ich will nicht den Tod der Ärzte – ich will meine Freiheit haben!"[178]

XXIV

O diese Lust, immer neu, aus gelockertem Lehm!
Niemand beinah hat den frühesten Wagern geholfen.
Städte entstanden trotzdem an beseligten Golfen,
Wasser und Öl füllten die Krüge trotzdem.

Götter, wir planen sie erst in erkühnten Entwürfen,
die uns das mürrische Schicksal wieder zerstört.
Aber sie sind die Unsterblichen. Sehet, wir dürfen
jenen erhorchen, der uns am Ende erhört.

Wir, ein Geschlecht durch Jahrtausende: Mütter und
    Väter,
immer erfüllter von dem künftigen Kind,
daß es uns einst, übersteigend, erschüttere, später.

Wir, wir unendlich Gewagten, was haben wir Zeit!
Und nur der schweigsame Tod, der weiß, was wir sind
und was er immer gewinnt, wenn er uns leiht.

This sonnet, linking with the preceding one, continues the idea of dare and danger. If the emphasis in the last sonnet was on "Gefahr", on the idea of living in danger, unprotected but by the same token free, here the emphasis is on the "dared ones", on the human race and all that it has "nevertheless", "trotzdem", achieved. In the Seventh and Ninth Elegies the Angel is proudly shown the things created by man and similarly here, in this single-minded and smoothly-running poem, reviewing the course of history, the irrepressible productivity and creativity of man is celebrated, the cities and civilisations it has brought forth, the immortal gods it has projected, for ever outlasting and surpassing itself in new generations. That God, the gods, are daring designs of man is a persistent Rilke theme and often this can seem close to a Feuerbach style of atheism. To Lotte Hepner he wrote:

> Könnte man die Geschichte Gottes nicht behandeln als einen gleichsam nie angetretenen Teil des menschlichen Gemütes, einen immer aufgeschobenen, aufgesparten, schließlich versäumten ...[179]

Yet there are few bodies of poetry in which the idea of God is so prominent and insistent. Let none of the gods pass away; they are all still necessary and valid, he writes in that February of 1922:

> Keiner der Götter vergeh. Wir brauchen sie alle und jeden,
> jeder gelte uns noch, jedes gestaltete Bild.[180]

To his pastor friend, Rudolf Zimmermann, he says he would wish to be able to worship in all temples.[181] If this has led to the pious tone in much of the more hagiographical literature on Rilke, it has also irritated many readers, who feel that Rilke is taking the name of God in vain, exploiting the associations of something he does not believe in. But then Rilke does not come to any "atheistic" conclusion, neither in the *Sonnets* nor anywhere else. It is clear that he reacted against the religion of his childhood, which worshipped an other-world God at the expense of the earth. To Pastor Zimmermann he also wrote how the "detachment" and "hereafterness" of God had disturbed him from childhood:

> Die Abgetrenntheit, die endgültig gewordene Jenseitigkeit Gottes erstaunte und beunruhigte mich, seit ich ein Kind war.[182]

What is expressed here in more diplomatically generalised terms is expressed with the full force of a feeling of personal betrayal in poems like "Arme Heilige aus Holz", on the wooden saints to whom his mother brought the flowers he should have had,[183] or the following bitter poem:

Ach wehe, meine Mutter reißt mich ein.
Da hab ich Stein auf Stein zu mir gelegt,
und stand schon wie ein kleines Haus, um das sich
groß der Tag bewegt,
sogar allein.
Nun kommt die Mutter, kommt und reißt mich ein.

Sie reißt mich ein, indem sie kommt und schaut.
Sie sieht es nicht, daß einer baut.
sie geht mir mitten durch die Wand von Stein.
Ach wehe, meine Mutter reißt mich ein.

Die Vögel fliegen leichter um mich her.
Die fremden Hunde wissen: das ist *der*.
Nur einzig meine Mutter kennt es nicht,
mein langsam mehr gewordenes Gesicht.

Von ihr zu mir war nie ein warmer Wind.
Sie lebt nicht dorten, wo die Lüfte sind.
Sie liegt in einem hohen Herz-Verschlag
und Christus kommt und wäscht sie jeden Tag.[184]

Reacting to this betrayal, he is determined, he says later, not to cede to God any of life's potentialities:

... keinerlei Lebenspotenzen von jetzt an Gott abzutreten, ja gerade die intensivsten und rätselhaftesten hier zu behalten.[185]

In a long letter in 1923 he elaborates on his use of the term "God" and writes:

Jetzt würdest Du mich ihn kaum je nennen hören, es ist eine unbeschreibliche Diskretion zwischen uns, und wo einmal Nähe war und Durchdringung, da spannen sich neue Fernen ... Das Faßliche entgeht, verwandelt sich, statt des Besitzes erlernt man den Bezug, und es entsteht eine Namenlosigkeit, die wieder bei Gott beginnen muß, um vollkommen und ohne Ausrede zu sein ... die Eigenschaften werden

> Gott, dem nicht mehr Sagbaren, abgenommen,
> fallen zurück an die Schöpfung, an Liebe und
> Tod ... und alles tief und innig Hiesige, das die
> Kirche ans Jenseits veruntreut hat, kommt
> zurück; alle Engel entschließen sich, lobsingend
> zur Erde![186]

As far as Rilke's own belief is concerned, it is probably the word "Bezug" here rather than the name of God that is at its centre. The devout wish is to establish a relationship with a whole that includes here and beyond, life and death. In that letter to Lotte Hepner in 1915, in which he surmises that the history of God might be regarded as an untrodden region of humanity, he suggests that death was similarly excluded from our lives:

> Gott und Tod waren nun draußen, waren das
> Andere, und das Eine war unser Leben, das nun
> um [den] Preis dieser Ausscheidung menschlich
> zu werden schien, vertraulich, möglich, leistbar,
> in einem geschlossenen Sinn das Unsrige.

But this is in the end, he feels, to fly in the face of Nature, which knows nothing of such suppression, repression, "Verdrängung":

> ... blüht ein Baum, so blüht so gut der Tod in
> ihm wie das Leben, und der Acker ist voller Tod,
> der aus seinem liegenden Gesicht einen reichen
> Ausdruck des Lebens treibt, und die Tiere gehen
> geduldig von einem [zum] anderen – und überall
> um uns ist der Tod noch zu Haus und aus den
> Ritzen der Dinge sieht er uns zu, und ein
> rostiger Nagel, der irgendwo aus einer Planke
> steht, tut Tag und Nacht nichts, als sich freuen
> über ihn.

Finally he recommends the reading of Tolstoy, who had thought so deeply, so "purely" about death. He extols Tolstoy as one of those who live out of a sense of the whole. The passage encapsulates both Rilke's ideal of wholeness and his bitterness towards the dregs of religious belief with its purely negative death and its spurious consolations:

> Sein enormes Naturerleben (ich weiß kaum einen Menschen, der so leidenschaftlich in die Natur eingelassen war) setzte ihn erstaunlich in den Stand, aus dem Ganzen heraus zu denken und zu schreiben, aus einem Lebensgefühl, das vom feinverteiltesten Tode so durchdrungen war, daß er überall mit enthalten schien, als ein eigentümliches Gewürz in dem starken Geschmack des Lebens –, aber gerade deshalb konnte dieser Mensch so tief, so fassungslos erschrecken, wenn er gewahrte, daß es irgendwo den puren Tod gab, die Flasche voll Tod oder diese häßliche Tasse mit dem abgebrochenen Henkel und der sinnlosen Aufschrift "Glaube, Liebe, Hoffnung", aus der einer Bitternis des unverdünnten Todes zu trinken gezwungen war.[187]

The same ideas recur in what is perhaps the bitterest of all his poems, "Der Tod" contrasting the false death in all its ugly imagery of an outworn faith and senseless babble with the natural phenomenon of the falling star. That concluding image recalls the sight of a falling star, seen from a bridge in Toledo, which he describes in a letter in January 1919. The star seemed to fall through his "inner space" as well as through outer space – one of several occasions in which Rilke believed he had experienced a sense of universal unity and, as he says in that letter, "one single undifferentiated space".

> Da steht der Tod, ein bläulicher Absud
> in einer Tasse ohne Untersatz.
> Ein wunderlicher Platz für eine Tasse:
> steht auf dem Rücken einer Hand. Ganz gut
> erkennt man noch an dem glasierten Schwung
> den Bruch des Henkels. Staubig. Und: >*Hoff-nung*<
> an ihrem Bug in aufgebrauchter Schrift.

> Das hat der Trinker, den der Trank betrifft,
> bei einem fernen Frühstück ab-gelesen.
>
> Was sind denn das für Wesen,
> die man zuletzt wegschrecken muß mit Gift?
>
> Blieben sie sonst? Sind sie denn hier vernarrt
> in dieses Essen voller Hindernis?
> Man muß ihnen die harte Gegenwart
> ausnehmen, wie ein künstliches Gebiß.
> Dann lallen sie. Gelall, Gelall ...
>
> ...
>
> O Sternenfall,
> von einer Brücke einmal eingesehn –:
> Dich nicht vergessen. Stehn![188]

The rejection of Christian religion and its partialities and the resolve to be steadfast in his own creed of wholeness, these are clear enough in Rilke, but much remains a mystery and in the end, like the ending of this sonnet, more agnostic than anything else. This sonnet on "us", the generations of human beings, begins by referring to us as "darers", but ends with a reference to us as "dared ones" and the suggestion of an unfathomed force behind our existence. The idea of "Wagnis" clearly relates to that other concept of "Gefahr". The only fulfillment is relationship to the whole, unprotected by the partialities of any creed that would exclude perils, above all the peril of death. One of the last translations of this central creed into pure poetry is the last answering poem to Erika Mitterer on the 24th August 1926, with its images of the far-flung ball that is "gewagt" and the dove leaving the dovecote that is "gefährdet", both, by being dared and endangered, infinitely enriched.[189]

In this celebration of safety in danger, of the natural wholeness which alone can give total security, man is most usually seen as recalcitrant and in denial.

But, just as in the *Elegies*, the same consciousness that seems to exclude man and make of his existence an eternal leave-taking and "Gegenübersein" is seen to serve a purpose in a more intense internalisation, so too human consciousness can, if man is wholly affirmative, serve to make the human being even more "daring" than Nature itself. In one of those late dedicatory poems, in which he so often seems to summarise the "intention" of his poetry, this one dating from June 1924, he writes:

> Wie die Natur die Wesen überläßt
> dem Wagnis ihrer dumpfen Lust und keins
> besonders schützt in Scholle und Geäst:
> so sind auch wir dem Urgrund unseres Seins
> nicht weiter lieb; er wagt uns. Nur daß wir,
> mehr noch als Pflanze oder Tier,
> mit diesem Wagnis gehn; es wollen; manchmal auch
> wagender sind (und nicht aus Eigennutz)
> als selbst das Leben ist –, um einen Hauch
> wagender ... Dies schafft uns, außerhalb von Schutz,
> ein Sichersein, dort wo die Schwerkraft wirkt
> der reinen Kräfte; was uns schließlich birgt
> ist unser Schutzlossein und daß wir's so
> in's Offne wandten, da wir's drohen sahen,
> um es, im weitsten Umkreis, irgendwo,
> wo das Gesetz uns anrührt, zu bejahen.[190]

In this affirmation of an unprotected totality Rilke is uncompromising and unambiguous, but that does not lessen the sense of mystery. This is still the poetry of myth and mystery, of Angel and Orpheus, of God and the gods, of the Immortal Ones as in this sonnet. For just as the end is left open in the *Elegies* in the mission of transformation into ourselves –

> in –
> o unendlich
> – in uns! wer wir am Ende auch seien

– here too the last word is given to "taciturn death":

> Und nur der schweigsame Tod, der weiß, was wir sind
> und was er immer gewinnt, wenn er uns leiht.

There is an ambiguity in these last lines in that "uns" can be understood as accusative or dative, that is to say either in the sense that death lends us (to life) or that death lends (life) to us. The accusative seems more likely, but in either case the main sentiment of the sonnet is the same, that human history is gainful, a "Gewinn", though what that profit is and what we are, "was wir sind", remains as shrouded in mystery as in the *Elegies:* "was wir am Ende auch seien".

XXV

> Schon, horch, hörst du der ersten Harken
> Arbeit; wieder den menschlichen Takt
> in der verhaltenen Stille der starken
> Vorfrühlingserde. Unabgeschmackt
>
> scheint dir das Kommende. Jenes so oft
> dir schon Gekommene scheint dir zu kommen
> wieder wie Neues. Immer erhofft,
> nahmst du es niemals. Es hat dich genommen.
>
> Selbst die Blätter durchwinterter Eichen
> scheinen im Abend ein künftiges Braun.
> Manchmal geben sich Lüfte ein Zeichen.
>
> Schwarz sind die Sträucher. Doch Haufen von Dünger
> lagern als satteres Schwarz in den Aun.
> Jede Stunde, die hingeht, wird jünger.

This nature-poem is one of the most uncomplicated of the cycle. According to Rilke himself it is a "companion-piece to the Children's Spring-Song of the First Part of the *Sonnets*".[191] Reminiscent of the earlier "Dinggedichte", it is, from the opening injunction to "hearken, hear the harrows" and with its deliberately laboured rhythm, an effectively concrete celebration of the ever familiar and yet ever new miracle of Spring. "The mystery and miracle of the return of spring, the gradual Northern spring, expected and yet always unexpected, was perhaps of all natural phenomena the one which Rilke most deeply felt", says Leishman, reminding us of other spring poems like "Vorfrühling" or "Schon kehrt der Saft aus einer Allgemeinheit".[192] These are late poems, from 1924, and the letters of his last years speak most nostalgically of the coming and promise of spring. In his last year he writes of the call of the cuckoo:

Ah! welche Leichtigkeit, welche wunderbare
Leichtigkeit des Vogels, der verspricht,
verspricht, zu viel verspricht.[193]

XXVI

Wie ergreift uns der Vogelschrei ...
Irgend ein einmal erschaffenes Schreien.
Aber die Kinder schon, spielend im Freien,
schreien am wirklichen Schreien vorbei.

Schreien den Zufall. In Zwischenräume
dieses, des Weltraums, (in welchen der heile
Vogelschrei eingeht, wie Menschen in Träume –)
treiben sie ihre, des Kreischens, Keile.

Wehe, wo sind wir? Immer noch freier,
wie die losgerissenen Drachen
jagen wir halbhoch, mit Rändern von Lachen,

windig zerfetzten. – Ordne die Schreier,
singender Gott! daß sie rauschend erwachen,
tragend als Strömung das Haupt und die Leier.

Human disruptiveness begins already in childhood. The Eighth Elegy spoke of the child as sometimes totally open and totally absorbed. But the Eighth Elegy also says the child is soon forced to turn around, look backwards, away from openness:

> ... denn schon das frühe Kind
> wenden wir um und zwingens, daß es rückwärts
> Gestaltung sehe, nicht das Offne ...

Here, in this sonnet, too, children already interrupt the pure, necessary cries of nature with the dissonance of human chance and discord, the poem ending with the appeal to Orpheus to order their lives, make of them a stream that bears his music, as the head and lyre of Orpheus were borne to Lesbos in the mythical story. As often with Rilke, one may well be in two minds reading this poem, in which the human voice drives a wedge through the harmony of nature. On the one hand, sceptical, both about the ideally untroubled world, the "heile Welt", and about that obsessive prejudice against rational human attitudes – dreaming men are different, the poem suggests – and at the same time admire the way in which the poem conveys what is jagged and tattered, not only by the imagery, but in the almost shrill sound effects, the convoluted and as it were wedged together syntax.

XXVII

Giebt es wirklich die Zeit, die zerstörende?
Wann, auf dem ruhenden Berg, zerbricht sie die Burg?
Dieses Herz, das unendlich den Göttern gehörende,
wann vergewaltigts der Demiurg?

Sind wir wirklich so ängstlich Zerbrechliche,
wie das Schicksal uns wahr machen will?
Ist die Kindheit, die tiefe, versprechliche,
in den Wurzeln – später – still?

Ach, das Gespenst des Vergänglichen,
durch den arglos Empfänglichen
geht es, als wär es ein Rauch.

Als die, die wir sind, als die Treibenden,
gelten wir doch bei bleibenden
Kräften als göttlicher Brauch.

One of the most impressive sonnets, this is closely related to the *Elegies* and in particular to the Ninth Elegy and to the function of man as defined in the Hulewicz letter. It takes up the theme of transitoriness and asks if the heart of man will be ravished, the fortress of the human heart pillaged by time the destroyer, the demiurge, the deity that, according to Plato, made the material world. In gnostic tradition time was created not by the good gods, but by the more malevolent demiurges. Most critics, as Mörchen notes, read the sonnet as expressing in some sense a faith in indestructibility (Geering, Albert-Lasard, Kretschmar, Rehm, to some extent Buddeberg. Here, as elsewhere, Mason is more cautious, always stressing the troubled, uncertain element in Rilke – too many critics, he suggests, ignore Rilke's question-marks.) Möhrchen himself goes to the other extreme. While most critics, in particular Holthusen, to whom Mörchen is most opposed, but also Geering, Kippenberg, Bollnow, Kohlschmidt, Buddeberg, understand the third stanza in the sense that the spectre of mutability is dissolved, Mörchen flatly disagrees. For him the function of the smoke image is in no way to banish the spectre image, but means rather the clouding, obscuring, dulling of any pure existence, "Vernebelung und Trübung des reinen Seins".[194] But this surely runs counter to the obvious sense of the third stanza as conveyed in Leishman's translation:

> Ah, Mutability's spectre!
> out through the simple accepter
> you, like a vapour recede.

Not that that disposes of the difficulties; for the real difficulty is not in understanding what Rilke is saying, but the difficulty of what he proposes, of being indeed "guilelessly receptive", for it is on this that all depends. Here as elsewhere in Rilke it is the attitude that matters and he seems to maintain that one can indeed be so receptive to existence as to recognise and experience the life and death unity. But the receptivity must be "arglos", a word to which he gives extraordinary weight, meaning guileless, innocent, unsuspecting and – "arg" meaning evil – in a sense a see-no-evil attitude, not thinking ill of life, unsuspicious. It is easy to understand how this can be seen to be uncritical, irrational even and an unhuman attitude. But Rilke insists on the possibility and validity of this guileless receptivity that enables us to experience a wholeness of existence. In his note to this sonnet, Leishman, who says that he translates "Vergängliches" as "mutability", as a deliberate echo of Spenser's *Cantos of Mutabilitie*, compares the spectre of mutability theme in Tennyson and in Rilke:

> Tennyson could only get rid of the "spectre" through his belief in personal immortality; Rilke would have us get rid of it by entering what he calls the *pure relation*, where life and death, present and past, are felt to be continuous and one; by becoming simply, guilelessly receptive, renouncing all personal claims, surrendering ourselves completely to the influence of powers we hold to be divine.

This guileless receptivity is, in Rilke's poetry, something once for all experienced in childhood. That childhood survives and sustains us is one of his basic experiences. That unfinished elegy begins:

> Laß dir, daß Kindheit war, diese namenlose
> Treue der Himmlischen, nicht widerrufen vom
>   Schicksal;
> ... Denn zeitlos
> hält sie das Herz.

> Don't let the fact that childhood once was, that nameless bond between Heaven and us, be revoked by fate ... For timelessly it holds the heart.

And the Ninth Elegy ends:

> Siehe, ich lebe. Woraus? Weder Kindheit noch
>   Zukunft
> werden weniger ... Überzähliges Dasein
> entspringt mir im Herzen.

In the Leishman/Spender translation:

> Look, I am living. On what? Neither childhood nor future
> are growing less ... Supernumerous existence
> wells up in my heart.

And, as also in the Ninth Elegy, the sonnet, too, suggests for man a purpose in the very intensity with which he experiences mutability, fulfilling a celestial need. The last word of the sonnet, "Brauch", has a multiplicity of meanings, custom, tradition, use etc., with the associations both of "brauchen" and of "gebrauchen", but the primary sense would seem to be a sense of fulfilling a purpose.

XXVIII

O komm und geh. Du, fast noch Kind, ergänze
für einen Augenblick die Tanzfigur
zum reinen Sternbild einer jener Tänze,
darin wir die dumpf ordnende Natur

vergänglich übertreffen. Denn sie regte
sich völlig hörend nur, da Orpheus sang.
Du warst noch die von damals her Bewegte
und leicht befremdet, wenn ein Baum sich lang

besann, mit dir nach dem Gehör zu gehn.
Du wußtest noch die Stelle, wo die Leier
sich tönend hob –; die unerhörte Mitte.

Für sie versuchtest du die schönen Schritte
und hofftest, einmal zu der heilen Feier
des Freundes Gang und Antlitz hinzudrehn.

The sonnet is a tribute to Wera, the girl to whom the *Sonnets to Orpheus* are dedicated, and to the art of rhythmical movement that responds to Orpheus and, like Orpheus himself – or the God of the *Stundenbuch* – "comes and goes", moves between world and otherworld. Like many of the gods and heroes of mythology, the figuration of her dance is imagined as turned into a constellation. According to the myth, nature itself came to Orpheus in response to his music, but she is even more immediately responsive and said to be "slightly disconcerted" if nature – like the tree in the opening sonnet – is slower in entering the sense of sound. When it is said that her dance is such as those in which we surpass nature "in a transitory manner", "vergänglich", the term probably relates to that theme of man's function, meaning, therefore, not so much briefly or momentarily, as rather: by virtue of the consciousness of mutability. (The subject "sie" in the fifth line refers to nature, not the girl.) Finally it is suggested that, initiated as she is into the very heart of orphic mystery – we can imagine her as a priestess of

Orpheus – she danced and hoped that one day she would lead the friend, presumably the poet himself, to the sacred celebration, in other words be the inspiration for these sonnets.

XXIX

Stiller Freund der vielen Fernen, fühle,
wie dein Atem noch den Raum vermehrt.
Im Gebälk der finstern Glockenstühle
laß dich läuten. Das, was an dir zehrt,

wird ein Starkes über dieser Nahrung.
Geh in der Verwandlung aus und ein.
Was ist deine leidendste Erfahrung?
Ist dir Trinken bitter, werde Wein.

Sei in dieser Nacht aus Übermaß
Zauberkraft am Kreuzweg deiner Sinne,
ihrer seltsamen Begegnung Sinn.

Und wenn dich das Irdische vergaß,
zu der stillen Erde sag: Ich rinne.
Zu dem raschen Wasser sprich: Ich bin.

The reference in the preceding sonnet to the friend leads over into this last sonnet, which according to Rilke's note, is addressed "to a friend of Wera", so, one can assume, to himself, in the universal sense of the poet's self-address, which can also be said to be a final address to the reader.[195] The cycle ends, as the second part began, with the motif of breathing, breathing as interchange and enlargement of space and transformed into a poem. It relates to that idea of the function of human life enriching the space that "consumes" it – the same term, "zehren", as in the First Elegy. Most translations translate the opening phrase as "silent friend", but the original suggests not so much silent as quiet, with the stillness of rest and receptivity. The whole poem suggests a restful conclusion, an acceptance of the darkness of destiny, or an encouragement to accept transformation and be transformed ino harmony, like the bell in the sombre belfry, in all the darkness that surrounds us. In one of his letters Rilke describes a bell tower on a lake island and how it:

> Zeit und Schicksal hinausläutet über den See, als ob er die Sichtbarkeit aller hier aufgegebenen Leben in sich zusammenfaßte und immer wieder ihr Vergängliches unsichtbar, in der sonoren Verwandlung der Töne, in den Raum hinübergäbe.[196]

The most summary admonition in the cycle is doubtless the line: "Geh in der Verwandlung aus und ein", recalling the sentiment of several earlier sonnets, more especially "Wolle die Wandlung" and "Sei allem Abschied voran". The following lines, with their echo perhaps of the cross-roads image of human discord in the third sonnet, call on the magical orphic powers of the protagonist to give sense to the human senses, to be, as it were, an equal partner of the earth, equally in motion, equally at rest. In an essay on Countess de Noailles, Rilke wrote on those lover-poetesses in the tradition of Sappho and says of the soul of such a lover-poetess:

> Diese Seele nimmt alles auf sich. Sie heißt das Weitoffensein des Herzens gut ... Es ist eine naive äolische Seele, die sich nicht schämt, dort zu wohnen, wo die Sinne sich kreuzen, und die nichts entbehrt, weil diese enfalteten Sinne einen Kreis bilden, der keine Lücke hat: so weilt sie im Bewußtsein einer ununterbrochenen Welt.[197]

Something like this "consciousness of an uninterrupted world" is probably, with the help of the orphic myth, what Rilke invokes, or hopes to evoke in the *Sonnets to Orpheus*.

The demand that he hereby makes on the reader is resisted by some critics, reacting against the cult of Rilke as religious leader rather than as craftsman poet. But there is no doubt that Rilke makes large claims – whether religious is the right term for them or not – for his poetry, for poetry *per se*. It may be that, as Eliot suggests, there is no easy equation between poetry and belief, but Rilke would seem to claim a reality for his orphic mythology, much as the Baroque poet claims to mean the one true God and no "mere metaphor, decked out with poetic finery" –

> Nicht durch ein Gleichnis nuhr
> noch schöne Poeterey
> Geziret und gefüllt mit künsten mancherley.
> Sondern der wahre Gott
> des Vatters eynigr Sohn ...[198]

If in the mediaeval tradition Christ is the *verus Orpheus*, there is a sense in which Rilke is reinstating Orpheus as the true divinity for that "open" attitude and "relationship" to a "whole" he claims to have achieved.

The recurring motif of praise, as in the much anthologised:

> Oh sage, Dichter, was du tust?
>   – Ich rühme.
> Aber das Tödliche und Ungetüme,
> wie hältst du's aus, wie nimmst du's hin
>   – Ich rühme. ...

is the simplest expression – though it makes the most difficult demands and can have many questionable aspects – of that "Affirmation of All" or what the editors of the annotated edition call his "Ontodizee".[199] It is a creed drawn from his experience of art, not just the fact of composition, but the affirmative nature of art as he experiences it, just as he speaks of rhyme as a goddess, an infinitely affirmative yes:

> C'est une très grande déesse, la divinité de coincidences
> très secrètes et très anciennes ... La vraie rime n'est pas
> un moyen de la poésie, c'est un 'oui' infinement
> affirmatif.[200]

It is not that he idolises art in any *l'art pour l'art* fashion, or that he in any way isolates it. On the contrary, when he stands in front of Rembrandt's *The Blinding of Samson*, with its transformation into art of such terrible subject-matter, the question he asks himself is: is there in life, too, something similar, a vantage-point such as that of the artist, which, for the sake of completeness, can, like God, accommodate all?

> Was ist das? Gibt es im Leben ähnliches? Gibt es
> Herzverhältnisse, die das Grausamste einschließen, um
> der Vollzähligkeit willen, weil die Welt doch erst Welt
> ist, wenn *Alles* darin geschieht; ich konnte mir Gott
> immer nur als Den denken, der *Alles* zuläßt ...[201]

Rejecting the redemption claims of the faith he was brought up in, as he reacted against what he felt to be its repressiveness, Rilke lived by this creed derived from his art, just as in the practical sense of his day-to-day needs he lived, if not uniquely, certainly very unusually, solely on his poetry.

It may be the very urgency and existential commitment of this more-than-mere-poetry attitude that makes some readers uncomfortable with Rilke's ideas. And there are moral arguments, perhaps irrefutable ones, against his "Ontodizee" – as marshalled, for example, by Egon Schwarz in *Das verschluckte Schluchzen*. And yet his work is extraordinarily impressive as poetry and challenging as a credo. Of course it is the force of the poetry itself that carries conviction and this is probably lost in the very act of explicating texts, which is rather like constantly interrupting a musical composition. Probably the best commentary on the *Sonnets* would be an uninterrupted reading of a poem such as the Elegy for Marina Zwetajewa-Efron, which seems to encapsulate his creed. In his last year, that year of almost constant pain, he received a letter from

Boris Pasternak, whom he had known as a boy in Russia, expressing not only his own admiration, but that of another Russian poet, Marina Zwetajewa, living in exile in Paris, and asking Rilke as a favour to send her some of his work. Indeed Marina did not so much admire Rilke as idolize him. Orpheus, she writes to a friend, has appeared again, this time in Germany. Rilke was not just a poet, but, as she says in German "Geist der Dichtung", and again: "Dichtung an sich". "Rilke ist ein Mythos, der Beginn eines neuen Mythos vom nachkommenden Gott", she writes. (In the last weeks of his illness her excesses and, doubtless, her possessiveness, were more than he could cope with.)[202] Pasternak's request started a correspondence, which included the Elegy, related by title to the Duino cycle, but in a post-elegiac mode. The beginning of that poem may serve to sum up the spirit that informs the *Sonnets to Orpheus*:

> O die Verluste ins All, Marina, die stürzenden Sterne!
> Wir vermehren es nicht, wohin wir uns werfen, zu welchem
> Sterne hinzu! Im Ganzen ist immer schon alles gezählt.
> So auch, wer fällt, vermindert die heilige Zahl nicht.
> Jeder verzichtende Sturz stürzt in den Ursprung und heilt.
> Wäre denn alles ein Spiel, Wechsel des Gleichen, Verschiebung,
> nirgends ein Name und kaum irgendwo heimisch Gewinn?
> Wellen, Marina, wir Meer! Tiefen, Marina, wir Himmel,
> Erde, Marina, wir Erde, wir tausendmal Frühling, wie Lerchen,
> die ein ausbrechendes Lied in die Unsichtbarkeit wirft.
> Wir beginnens als Jubel, schon übertrifft es uns völlig;
> plötzlich, unser Gewicht dreht zur Klage abwärts den Sang.
> Aber auch so: Klage? Wäre sie nicht: jüngerer Jubel nach unten?
> Auch die unteren Götter wollen gelobt sein, Marina.
> So unschuldig sind Götter, sie warten auf Lob wie die Schüler.
> Loben, du Liebe, laß uns verschwenden mit Lob ...[203]

This might be translated:

> Oh the losses into the All, Marina, the precipitate stars!
> We can't increase it, wherever we plunge, to whichever
> Star we may come! In the Whole all is already accounted.
> Every relinquishing fall falls to the source and is healed.
> Is it all then a game, change of the same, a displacement,
> Nowhere a name and scarcely a gain of our own?
> Waves, Marina, we are ocean! Depths, Marina, we are sky.
> Earth, Marina, we are earth, a thousand times Spring, like larks,
> That a song bursting forth from them flings out of sight.
> We begin it as jubilation, already it wholly exceeds us;
> All of a sudden our weight bends the song down to lament.
> And yet even so: is not lament a younger, downwardly jubilation?
> Even the gods below want to be praised, Marina.
> Gods are such innocent beings, waiting like pupils for praise.
> Praising, my dearest, let us be spendthrift with praise.

The "meaning" of the *Sonnets to Orpheus* is at once simple and complex. Simple in the sense that what Orpheus stands for is that all-embracing praise of creation –

> Rühmen, das ists! Ein zum Rühmen Bestellter (1,7) –

which is indeed no less the purport of the *Elegies* and was so from the beginning, for the opening lines of the last Elegy –

> Daß ich dereinst, an dem Ausgang der grimmigen Einsicht,
> Jubel und Ruhm aufsinge zustimmenden Engeln –

date from the inception of the *Elegies* in 1912 in Duino. But it is also a highly complex and controversial meaning. Rilke himself has told us that the most valid sonnet is the Thirteenth Sonnet of the second part, and its concluding exhortation, once again of praise and jubilation, encapsulates that complexity:

> Zu dem gebrauchten sowohl, wie zum dumpfen und stummen
> Vorrat der vollen Natur, den unsäglichen Summen,
> zähle dich jubelnd hinzu und vernichte die Zahl.

The most ardent admirer of Rilke must admit that this "destruction of number" has many questionable aspects, having to do with Rilke's distrust of rationalising and moralising, almost one might say distrust of the adult world with its judgements and prescriptions in favour of an undifferentiating "Ontodizee". But in the same breath that he "destroys the account" he counts himself in, into this altogether-to-be-affirmed creation. He sustains this attitude not only with extraordinary force in his poetry, but one might truly say with heroic consistency in his life.

Notes

1. In his preference for the latest, "less portentous" and "more open" Rilke, Mason also anticipates a point made in the annotated edition. Mason wrote: "What is true of the *Sonnets to Orpheus* is true ... in the main of all Rilke's later poetry ... In its buoyant, song-like transparency and serenity, in its emotional and speculative fluidity and lightness the great bulk of this later lyric belongs to the sphere of the *Sonnets to Orpheus*, not of the *Duinese Elegies*". (Mason, *Rilke*, pp 106ff.) The editors of the annotated edition separate *Elegies* and *Sonnets*, associating the *Elegies* with the poems 1912 to 1922 and the *Sonnets* with the poems 1922 to 1926, although we tend to speak of *Elegies* and *Sonnets* in one breath. K.A. 2,703. It is true, of course, that *Elegies* and *Sonnets* do combine, since it was the experience of the *Elegies* that gave rise to the *Sonnets*.
2. Hermann Mörchen, *Rilkes Sonette an Orpheus*. Stuttgart 1958. Jacob Steiner, *Rilkes Duineser Elegien*. Bern 1962.
3. Rilke himself, who invariably refers to the *Sonnets* as a work he is only slowly coming to understand, most often speaks of understanding them in the act of reading them aloud. Cf. letters to Katharina Kippenberg, 21.3.1923 (KK p. 492), to Xaver von Moos, 20.4.1923 (Br. Number 385), to Gudi Nölke, 23.4.1923 (GN pp 113f.).
4. Timothy J. Casey, *Rainer Maria Rilke. A Centenary Essay.* London: 1976.
5. *Rainer Maria Rilke. Sonnets to Orpheus.* The German Text, with an English Translation, Introduction & Notes by J. B. Leishman. London: 1946
6. Edmond Jaloux, *La Dernière Amitié de R.M.Rilke.* Paris: 1949. pp 58f.
7. Br. 243 to Ilse Erdmann 11.9.1915. "... you must know that my feelings are not 'German', – in no way; even though I cannot be a stranger to the German spirit, since I am so rooted in its language, yet its manifestation today ... has brought me nothing but loathing and mortification; and still more the Austrian ... that I should ever feel at home in that is intellectually and emotionally quite impossible for me! How should I, whose heart has been formed by Russia, France, Italy, Spain, the desert and

the Bible, how should I be attuned to those whose boastful words surround me!"

[8] J. R. von Salis, *Rainer Maria Rilke Schweizerjahre*. Frauenfeld: 1952. p. 112.

[9] Br. 281, 15.2.1919.

[10] Kippenberg *op. cit*. p. 164.

[11] Br. 379 to Ilse Jahr, 22 February 1923. "I began with Things, which were the true confidants of my lonely childhood, and it was already a great achievement that, without any outside help, I managed to get as far as animals. But then Russia opened itself to me and granted me the brotherliness and the darkness of God, in whom alone there is community. That was what I *named* him then, the God who had broken in upon me, and for a long time I lived in the antechamber of his name ... Now you would hardly ever hear me name him; there is an indescribable discretion between us, and where nearness and penetration once were, new distances stretch forth ... instead of possession one learns relationship, and there arises a namelessness that must begin again with God, in order to be complete and without evasion".

[12] *Das Florenzer Tagebuch*, Frankfurt: 1942. p. 32. "Religion is the art of those who are uncreative. In prayer they become productive ... The non-artist must have a religion – in the profoundly inward sense – even if it only be one reposing on collective and historical convention. To be an atheist in his sense is to be a barbarian".

[13] Br. 21, 23 December 1903. "But if you recognise that God was not present in your childhood, nor before that, if you suspect that Christ was deluded by his yearning and Mohammed deceived by his pride; if you feel with alarm that he also does not exist now, at this hour in which we are speaking of him – what justification have you for missing him who never existed as though he had ceased to be, or for seeking him, as though he were lost? Why do you not think that he is the coming one, who has been impending from eternity, the future one, the final fruit of a tree of which we are the leaves?"

[14] Br. 364 to Lotti von Wedel, 26 May 1922. "A Fate that thinks and knows us ... yes, often one wishes to be strengthened and confirmed by such a one; but would it not immediately be at

the same time an onlooker, viewing us, with whom we would no longer be alone? The fact that we are enclosed in, dwell in a 'blind fate' is so to speak the condition after all of our own vision, of our viewing innocence. – It is only through the 'blindness' of our fate that we are profoundly related to the wonderful darkness of the world, that is to say to the Whole, to the incalculable that surpasses us".

[15] Babette Deutsch, *Poems from the Book of Hours,* London: 1947.

[16] *Rainer Maria Rilke. Prose and Poetry,* edited by Egon Schwarz. New York: 1991. p. 167.

[17] *The Book of Hours* translated by A. L. Peck, London: 1961.

[18] In the introduction to Peck's translation. Also, in German, in: Eudo C. Mason, *Exzentrische Bahnen,* Göttingen: 1963. p. 196.

[19] Klaus-Dieter Hähnel, *Rainer Maria Rilke Werk – Literaturgeschichte – Kunstanschauung.* Berlin and Weimar: 1984. pp 60ff.

[20] *The Best of Rilke* translated by Walter Arndt. Hanover and London: 1989.

[21] Br. A-S. pp 103f. "The incomparable value of these rediscovered Things lies in the fact that you can look at them as if they were completely unknown. No one knows what their intention is and (at least for the unscientific) no subject matter is attached to them, no irrelevant voice interrupts the silence of their concentrated reality ... no misunderstood fame colours their pure forms, no history casts a shadow over their naked clarity –: they are. That is all. This is how I see ancient art".

[22] Letter of 5 September 1902. *Briefe 1902–1906,* p 52.

[23] *Italienische Reise* 10 November and 2 December 1786.

[24] *The Selected Poetry of Rainer Maria Rilke* edited and translated by Stephen Mitchell. London: 1987.

[25] Fürstin Marie von Thurn und Taxis-Hohenlohe, *Erinnerungen an Rainer Maria Rilke.* München-Berlin: 1933. pp 40f. "Rilke told me later how these *Elegies* arose. He felt no premonition of what was being prepared within him ... he began to believe that this winter, too, would be without result. Then early one morning he received a troublesome business letter. He wanted to take care of it quickly and had to concern himself with numbers and other such dry matters. Outside a violent bora was

blowing, but the sea shone blue and silver. Rilke climbed down to the bastions, which, jutting out to the east and west, were connected by a narrow path at the foot of the castle. There the cliffs drop abruptly, for about 200 feet, into the sea. Rilke walked back and forth, completely lost in thought, for an answer to the letter absorbed him greatly. Then, all at once, in the midst of his brooding, he stopped, suddenly, for it seemed to him as if in the raging storm a voice had called to him: 'Who, if I cried, would hear me among the orders of angels?' Listening, he stood still. 'What is that?' he whispered, 'what is that coming?' He took his notebook, which he always had with him, and wrote down those words, together with a few lines that formed themselves without his intervention. Who came? He knew now: the God ... Calmly he climbed back up to his room, laid aside his notebook and took care of the business letter. But by evening the whole Elegy was written down. Shortly afterwards the second, the Angel-Elegy, was to follow".

[26] *The Foreign Gate* in: Sidney Keyes, *The Collected Poems*, London: 1945.

[27] *Rainer Maria Rilke. Poems 1906 to 1926*, translated by J. B. Leishman. Norfolk, Connecticut: 1957. p. 196.

[28] *Shakespeare and the Stoicism of Seneca.*

[29] *Rainer Maria Rilke. A Study of his Later Poetry* by Hans Egon Holthusen, translated by J. P. Stern. Cambridge: 1952. pp 42ff.

[30] Br. 346 "late in the evening of the ninth of February" 1922. "My dear friend, late and although I can barely manage to hold the pen, after several days of immense obedience in the spirit –, it must to *you* it must, now, before I try to sleep, be told: I have crossed the mountain! At last! The *Elegies* are there ... So. Dear friend, now I can breathe again and calmly go to something manageable. For this was larger than life –, during these days and nights I groaned as I did that time in Duino –, but even after that struggle there –, I did not know that *such* a storm of mind and heart could come over one! That one has endured it! that one has endured, Enough, it is there. I went out into the cold moonlight and stroked the little Muzot like a great animal – the ancient walls that granted this to me".

[31] *An Unofficial Rilke. Poems 1912–1926.* Selected, translated

and with an introduction by Michael Hamburger. London: 1981.

[32] See especially: Joachim Wolff, *Rilkes Grabschrift*. Heidelberg: 1983. Yeats' epitaph was inspired, or rather provoked, not so much by his reading of Rilke as by his misunderstanding of Rilke from what he had read about him. This and Rilke's epitaph is discussed in my essay: "Yeats and Rilke: Epitaphs in the Country Churchyards of Drumcliff and Raron" in: *Connections: Essays in Honour of Eda Sagarra*. Edited by Peter Skrine, Rosemary E. Wallbank-Turner and Jonathan West. Stuttgart: 1993.

[33] *Rilke Selected Poems* pp 39ff. There is also a translation by Stephen Spender in his *Collected Poems 1928–1953,* London: 1955. pp 205ff.

[34] In *Die deutsche Lyrik. Von der Spätromantik bis zur Gegenwart*, edited by Benno von Wiese. Düsseldorf: 1956. p. 324.

[35] Hans Berendt, *Rainer Maria Rilkes Neue Gedichte*, Bonn: 1957. p. 179.

[36] *The Odyssey* (Book XI). Translation by Walter Shewring. Oxford: 1980. p. 139.

[37] Buddeberg *op. cit.* p. 333

[38] Berendt *op. cit.* p. 183

[39] Paula Modersohn Becker, *Briefe und Tagebuchblätter*, München: n.d. (List Taschenbuch) p. 231. "When Otto's letters come to me, they are like a voice from the earth and I myself am like one who has died, who tarries in the Elysian Fields and hears this terrestrial cry".

[40] The translations from the *Elegies* are those by J. B. Leishman and Stephen Spender, published by the Hogarth Press, 3rd. edition, London: 1948.

[41] *The Iliad* (Book XVIII) Translated by Martin Hammond. (Penguin) London: 1987. p. 322.

[42] Romano Guardini, *Zu Rainer Maria Rilkes Deutung des Daseins* München: 1953. Also: Romano Guardini, *Rilke's Duino Elegies. An Interpretation.* Translated by K. G. Knight. London 1961.

[43] *Duineser Elegien* edited by E. L. Stahl, Oxford 1965. p. xxxi.

[44] Egon Schwarz, *Das verschluckte Schluchzen: Poesie und Politik bei Rainer Maria Rilke*. Frankfurt: 1972.

45   Dieter Bassermann, *Der späte Rilke* Essen and Freiburg i. Br.: 1948. Also, among several other publications: *Der andere Rilke*, Bad Homburg: 1961.
46   *Lettres françaises à Merline*, pp 18f.
47   *Tagebücher aus der Frühzeit*, p. 140.
48   Br. 410. Undated letter, posted 13 November 1925.
"*Affirmation of life-and-death turns out to be one in the Elegies* ... We must try to achieve the greatest possible consciousness of our existence, which is at home in *both these boundless realms, inexhaustibly nourished by both* ... *there is neither a this-world nor an other-world, but only the great unity* ... We of the here and now are not for a moment satisfied in the world of time, nor are we confined in it; we are continually over-flowing towards those who preceded us, towards our origin and towards those who seemingly come after us ... Transitoriness is everywhere plunging into a profound Being. And so all the manifestations of the here and now are not merely to be used in a time-limited way, but, so far as we can, set within those superior significances in which we share. *But not in the Christian sense* (from which I ever more passionately distance myself), but in a purely terrestrial, deeply terrestrial, blissfully terrestrial consciousness, what is needed is to provide the wider, the widest context for all that is *here* seen and touched. Not in a Beyond, whose shadow darkens the earth, but in a whole, *in the Whole* ... our task is to stamp this provisional, perishable earth into ourselves so deeply, so painfully and passionately, that its essence may rise again, "invisibly", in us. *We are the bees of the invisible. We passionately plunder the honey of the visible, to store it in the great golden hive of the invisible.* The *Elegies* show us at this task, this task of the continual conversion of the dear visible and tangible into the invisible vibration and agitation of our own nature ... If one makes the mistake of applying *Catholic* conceptions of death, of the hereafter, and of eternity to the *Elegies* or Sonnets, one is distancing oneself completely from their point of departure and preparing for oneself an ever more fundamental misunderstanding. The 'Angel' of the *Elegies* has nothing to do with the angel of the Christian heaven (rather with the angel figures of Islam) ... The Angel of the *Elegies* is that being in whom that transformation of the visible into the invisible we are

engaged in already appears completed ... *Elegies* and Sonnets
support each other constantly –, and I consider it an infinite grace
that, with the same breath, I was allowed to fill both these sails:
the little rust-coloured sail of the *Sonnets* and the *Elegies* gigantic
white canvas".

[49] To Irmela Linberg, 24.3 .1919. Schnack *op. cit.* p. 1380.

[50] K K. p. 455. 23 February 1923. "I keep calling them
sonnets. Although they are the freest and so to speak the most
modified that can be understood by that otherwise so sedate and
stable form. But precisely that; to play variations on the sonnet,
to lift it up and as it were carry it along at a run without
destroying it, was for me in this case a peculiar test and task;
about which, by the way, I had hardly to make up my mind. So
much did it set itself and bring its own solution along with it".

[51] Letter of 23 April 1923. Br. 386.

[52] Letter "an ein junges Mädchen", 20 November 1904. Br. 31.

[53] Letter of 3 August 1917. Unpublished, quoted, in English,
in Prater *op. cit.* p. 283. Rilke, as Leppmann notes (*op. cit.* esp. p.
250), admired Sophie Liebknecht, as he did Rosa Luxemburg,
though their ideology – which he probably never considered –
would be so alien to him.

[54] S. W. 2, p. 449.

[55] Letter of 19 October 1907. Br. 83.

[56] Letter of 11 February 1922. Br. 347.

[57] *Das tägliche Leben.* S.W. IV p. 893.

[58] Letter of 22. November 1920. Br. 303. "Art can only issue
from a purely anonymous centre".

[59] Letter to Nanny Wunderly-Volkart, 29 July 1920. Br. W-V.
1, p. 292. "... for ultimately there is only the one poet, that infinite
one, who makes himself felt, here and there through the ages, in
a mind that can surrender to him".

[60] Letter of 12 January 1922 to Robert Heygrodt. Br. 339.

[61] Letter of 25 November 1920. Br. 306. "For I have long
accustomed myself to view the things that are given to us
according to their intensity, without being concerned, as far as
that is humanly possible, about their duration, – in the end it is
the best and most discreet way of expecting *everything* from them
–, even duration".

[62] S. W. VI, p. 1127.

[63] Letter of 17 November 1912. Br. 174: Just now my feelings are more than ever one-sided, lament often predominates, but I know that one may make such full use of the strings of lament only if one is determined to play on them later, with their means, the whole jubilation that grows behind all that is borne, all the heaviness and pain, and without which jubilation the voices are incomplete".

[64] S. W.6, pp 924f.

[65] K. A. 1, pp 434, 890. *Briefe an Sidonie Nádherny*, p. 101.

[66] S. W. I, p. 772. "In the second stanza the graves are remembered in the famous old cemetery of Allyscamps near Arles, spoken of also in *Malte Laurids Brigge*".

[67] S. W. VI, p. 943. "Shall I imagine him in the soul-inhabited shade of Allyscamps, his glance pursuing a dragon-fly between those graves that are as open as the graves of the resurrected?"

[68] For example in the translations of Herter Norton, MacIntyre and Poulin.

[69] S. W. II, p. 259.

[70] S. W. VI, p. 1092.

[71] Letters of 12 April 1923 to Countess Sizzo and of 23 April 1923 to Clara. Br. 384 and 386.

[72] Letter to Alfred Schaer 26 February 1924. Br. 396.

[73] 22 May 1912. T.T. I p. 158

[74] 17 December 1912. Br. 178. "... where an ugly little bitch, highly pregnant, came to me; it was no noteworthy animal and doubtless full of chance progeny, about whom no fuss will have been made; but she came, when we were all alone, difficult as it was for her, came over to me and raised her great troubled eyes and besought me to look at her, – and in her own look there was truly everything that reaches beyond the individual, into I know not where, into the future or into the incomprehensible; and the resolution was that she got a lump of sugar from my coffee, but by the way, o so by the way, we so to speak said Mass together, the action was in itself nothing but a giving and a receiving, but the meaning and the gravity and our whole mutual understanding was boundless. After all that can only happen on earth, at all events it is good to have passed through here willingly, even if uncertainly, even if guiltily, even if no way

heroically – in the end one is marvellously prepared for divine circumstances".

75 Letter of 8 February 1912. Br. 154.
76 To Countess Sizzo, 1 June 1923. Br. 387. "In the poem *to the dog* what is meant by 'my master's hand' is the hand of the god, meaning here Orpheus. The poet will guide the hand, so that, for the sake of its infinite participation and devotion, it will bless the dog, which, almost like Esau, has put on his fell in order to share in its heart in a heritage, to which it does not have title, the whole heritage of human adversity and happiness".
77 Leisi p. 108.
78 Letters from Katharina Kippenberg 2 October 1915 and from Rilke 7 October 1915. Cp. Stahl *op. cit.* p. 308.
79 Peter Demetz: "In Sachen Rilke" in: *Insel Almanach auf das Jahr 1967* Frankfurt: 1966. p. 34.
80 S. W. VI, pp 726ff.
81 Letter of 11 February 1922. Br. 348.
82 K. A. p. 741.
83 S. W. 1, p. 772. Briefe aus Muzot, p. 99.
84 Br. 410.
85 Br. 338. "with this unity of the existent and abiding world, this affirmation towards life, this joyful, this emotional, this utterly competent belonging to the here and now – ah, only to the here and now?! No ... to the *whole,* to much more than the here and now. Oh, how, how she loved, how she reached with the antennae of her heart beyond all that is here tangible and comprehensible ..."
86 Br. 373. "am Dreikönigstag 1923".
87 The Sonnets translated by: Leishman, Young, Paulin, Herter Norton, MacIntyre , Norris and Keele.
88 *The Selected Poetry of Rainer Maria Rilke,* edited and translated by Stephen Mitchell. London 1987. p. 73.
89 K. A. 2, p. 745.
90 S. W. 2, p. 56.
91 S. W. 6, p. 829.
92 1 June 1923. Br. 387. "I believe that no poem in the *Sonnets* means anything that is not there fully written out, if to be sure often with its most discreet names. Anything in the nature of 'allusion' would, I am convinced, contradict the indescribable

being-there of the poem. So too in the unicorn no Christ-parallel is intended; but only all the love of the not-proven, ineffable, all the belief in the value and the reality of that which, through the centuries, our nature has created and extolled may be therein praised ...Truly the more tradition is for us outwardly restricted and confined, the more decisive it becomes for us, whether we are able to remain open and conductive to the most far-reaching and most secret traditions of humanity. The *Sonnets to Orpheus* are – so I more and more understand them – an effort in this profound direction carried out in ultimate obedience. The unicorn has all the connotations, ever and again celebrated in the middle ages, of virginity: hence it is said that it, the non-existent for the profane, is, as soon as it appears in the silver mirror held up to it by the virgin (see the tapestries of the XV century) and 'in her', as if in a second equally pure, equally secret mirror".

[93] S. W. 2, p. 258.

[94] Br. A.-S. pp 349f. "I am like the little anemone I once saw in the garden in Rome; throughout the day it had opened so wide that it could no longer shut at night-fall! It was frightful to see it in the dark meadow, wide open, still absorbing into its almost madly flung open calyx, and above it the far too large night that would not and would not be done. And near by all its prudent sisters, each closed up around its little measure of superfluity. I too am just so fatally turned outwards, and therefore distracted by everything, refusing nothing, my senses going across to every interruption without asking my leave; if there is a noise, I give myself up and *am* that noise; and, since everything, once it has adjusted to excitation, wants to be excited, I too, fundamentally, want to be disturbed, and am so without end".

[95] S. W. 1, pp 772f. "The rose of antiquity was a simple eglantine, red and yellow, in the colours that occur in flame. It blooms here, in the Valais, in certain gardens".

[96] S. W.2, p. 575.

[97] 11.9.1906. "... For to fade and to be faded and to yield oneself up to that is a further beauty beside the beauty of all that comes and burgeons and bears fruit ..."

[98] Sieber *op. cit.* pp 59 ff. "I often think of him and return

again and again to his image, which has remained indescribably moving for me. Much of "childhood", the sadness and helplessness of being a child, is embodied in his figure, in the ruff he wore, in the little neck, the chin, the beautiful brown eyes with their squint. So I evoked him once more in connection with the 8th. Sonnet, which expresses transitoriness, after he had already served as model in the 'Notebooks of M. L. Brigge', for little Erik Brahe, who died in childhood".

[99] Schmidt-Pauli *op. cit.* p. 20. "There Rilke stood still and pointed to a tree standing alone in the middle of the mown lawn. "Look – that is it, that is what I want and nothing else: I want to say that tree in such a manner that only the tree speaks in my words, as it is, with nothing of Rilke added. My poem 'The Ball' was completely successful in that respect. There I expressed nothing but the almost inexpressible reality of a pure movement – and hence it is my best poem".

[100] S. W. 1, p. 639.

[101] S. W. 2, p. 319. 24. August 1926.

[102] S. W. 2, p. 132.

[103] Br. A.-S pp 469, 634.

[104] S.W. 6, p. 776. "all of that has a tenacious immortality, a stubborn self-insistence, and, envious of all that is, clings to its own dreadful reality".

[105] Br. 373.

[106] S. W. 2, p. 267.

[107] S. W.1 p. 773. "Referring to the manner in which, according to ancient hunting custom, the peculiarly white rock-doves in certain districts of the Karst, by means of cloths carefully suspended into their caves and suddenly shaken in a particular way, are scared out of their subterranean dwellings to be shot during their terrified escape".

[108] Hattingberg, *op cit.*, pp 68, 136. "'But after all, what do we know', he concluded with a sigh, 'in the end does not everything reach beyond us, beyond our most inward and most insignificant, does not everything around us in the world have legality and validity even *without* us?'"

[109] S.W. 2, p. 188.

[110] Br. 253. "Our security must be somehow a relationship to

the whole, to a totality; to be secure means for us to become
aware of the innocence of injustice and to admit the formative
nature of suffering; means to reject names in order, behind them,
to give honour, as to guests, to all the unique forms and
combinations of fate ... means to suspect nothing, eject nothing ...
to give generous acceptance to insecurity ... in an infinite one,
security too will be infinite".

[111] Br. 10. "A great and eternal beauty goes through the whole
world and it is fairly spread over all things, small and great; for
in all that is important and essential there is no injustice in the
whole world".

[112] Br. 30. "And for the rest, let life happen. Believe me, life is,
at all events, in the right".

[113] S. W. 6, p. 1121. "One should endeavour in the case of
every power that claims a right over us to see all power, the
whole power, power itself, the power of God. One should say to
oneself that there is only *one* power and should *so* understand the
petty, false, flawed one as if it were that which rightly seizes
upon us. Would it not then lose its harmfulness? If one saw in
every power, even the wicked and malicious, always power
itself, I mean that which in the end has the right to be powerful,
would one not then withstand, unscathed so to speak, even the
unjust and the arbitrary?"

[114] Br. 405. "should fear and reject nothing so much as a
corrected world, in which the crooked are made straight and the
beggars enriched. The God of Totality sees to it that these
variations do not cease, and it would be the most superficial
attitude were one to regard the joy of the poet over this suffering
diversity as aesthetic excuse".

[115] *Der Erwählte.* Chapter: "Die Hochzeit".

[116] To Countess Dietrrichstein, 6. August 1919. Br. 287. "If
only man would desist from appealing to the cruelty in nature in
order to excuse his own! He forgets how infinitely innocently
even the most terrible in nature comes to pass, nature does not
look on, it has no distance, – in what is most dreadful it *is* totally,
its fruitfulness is in it, its magnaminity –; it is, if one may say so,
nothing but an expression of its fulness. Its consciousness
consists of its totality, because it contains *everything* it also
contains the cruel, – but man, who will never be able to

comprehend all, is never sure, whenever he chooses the terrible, let us say murder –, to contain as well the opposite of that abyss, and so his choice immediately passes judgement on him, since it makes him into an exception, an isolated, one-sided being, which is no longer attached to the whole. The good man, the purely decisive and capable man would not be able to exclude evil, disaster, suffering, misfortune, death from all the reciprocal cicumstances, but rather where such befell him, or he was the cause of such, he would stand there no different to someone subject to a visitation of nature, or himself a visitation against his will, he would be like the devastating stream, swollen by the torrential waters of the thaw, unable to shut himself off from their confluence".

[117] S. W. 2, p. 442.
[118] *loc. cit* 284f.
[119] 18. 3. 22. *Briefe aus Muzot* 133. "Today I am sending you only *one* of these sonnets, because, in the whole context, it is the one closest to me and ultimately the one that is most valid".
[120] 2.4.1922. KK. 461. "It includes all the others, and it expresses that which, though it still far exceeds me, my purest, most final achievement would someday, in the midst of life, have to be".
[121] Letter to Lotte Hepner 8 November 1915. Br. 247.
[122] In: *Wege zum Gedicht* edited by Rupert Hirschenauer and Albrecht Weber. München and Zürich: 1965. p. 296. "What else is Zahl but a principle of isolation, of multiplicity and division. In adding myself in I negate the number".
[123] To Countess Dietrichstein 9 October 1918. Br. 272.
[124] Letter of 30 January 1920. K.A.2, p. 754.
[125] S. W. 2, 97.
[126] S. W. 2, 100.
[127] Butler p. 357.
[128] Mörchen pp 471f. Angelloz, p. 289. Kretschmar, p. 63.
[129] Mörchen p. 321. S.W. 2, 520.
[130] 13.12.1900. *Tagebücher aus der Frühzeit*, p. 416.
[131] 3 February 1921. Br. 313.
[132] 6 September 1915. Br. 242. "It is only necessary that our eye should become a shade more perceptive, our ear more receptive, the taste of a fruit be absorbed more completely, smell

be more keenly endured, we need only be less forgetful and have greater presence of mind in touching and being touched, to receive from our most immediate experiences consolations that are more convincing, weightier, truer than all the suffering that can ever distress us".

[133] S. W. p. 467.

[134] *Die Briefe an Frau Gudi Nölke,* p. 196.

[135] Cf. Mörchen pp 331, 474f.

[136] Stahl, p. 319.

[137] Br. 405. "To wish to better somebody's situation is to present him, instead of difficulties to which he is accustomed and in which he is practised, with difficulties that find him perhaps more at a loss. If I was sometimes able to cast the imaginary voices of the dwarf or the beggar in the mould of my heart, the metal was not won from the wish that the dwarf or the beggar should have a less difficult lot; on the contrary, only through praising their incomparable fate could the poet, who had suddenly committed himself to them, be thorough and true, and he would have to fear and reject nothing so much as a corrected world, in which the dwarves are stretched and the beggars enriched. The God of Totality sees to it that these variations do not cease, and it would be the most superficial attitude were one to regard the joy of the poet over this suffering diversity as an aesthetic excuse ... In a world which endeavours to dissolve the divine in a kind of anonymity, that humanitarian overestimation is bound to find a place, which expects from human help what it is unable to give. And divine goodness is so indescribably bound up with divine severity, that an age which undertakes, anticipating providence, to dispense the former, replenishes at the same time the oldest stocks of cruelty. (We have experienced it.)"

[138] S. W. 2, 290.

[139] S. W. 1, 260.

[140] S. W. 2, 249.

[141] Leisi p. 159.

[142] S. W. 4, 695.

[143] Br. 9. "A togetherness of two people is an impossibility, and, where it nevertheless seems to be present, is a limitation, a mutual agreement which robs one or both of their fullest

freedom and development. But, provided there is an awareness that there can be infinite distances between even those who are closest to one another, a wonderful side by side relationship can develop, if they are able to cherish the distance between them, which gives them the possibility of seeing one another in full form and against the background of a vast heaven".

[144] S. W. 1, 622.

[145] 26 May 1922. Br. 364. "A Fate that thinks, that is aware of us, yes, one often wishes that one were strengthened and confirmed by such; but would it not be at the same time a Fate that sees us from without, that watches us, with which we would no longer be alone? That we are embedded in, dwell in, a 'blind fate' is, after all, the condition as it were of our own vision, of our watchful innocence. It is only through the 'blindness' of our fate that we relate so deeply to that which is so wonderfully muffled and opaque in the world, that is to say to the whole, to the incalculable that surpasses us".

[146] von Salis p. 40.

[147] 23 January 1924. S.W. 2,258.

[148] S. W. 2, p. 258. Leishman, in *Poems 1906 to 1926*, pp 289f. translates: "When from moments long unrecollected / rises in us what has long been mute, / fully-mastered, radiant, resurrected, / re-experienced in the Absolute: // there begins the word, as we conceive it; / us its value silently transcends. / For the spirit lonelying us intends / union through our fitness to achieve it".

[149] S. W. 2, 259f. Leishman translates *op. cit.* p. 298: "Happy who know that behind all speeches / still the unspeakable lies; / that it's from there that greatness reaches / us in the forms we prize! // Trusting not to the diversely fashioned / bridges of difference we outfling: / so that we gaze out of every impassioned / joy at some wholly communal thing".

[150] Letter to Ilse Jahr 22 February 1923. Br. 379.

[151] 31.March 1904. Br. A-S. pp 139f.

[152] S. W. 2, 118.

[153] Br. 127. "... this incomprehensible temple-world of Karnak, which, straightaway on the first evening and again yesterday in the light of a moon just beginning to wane, I saw, saw, saw – my God, one gathers one's senses, focusses one's eyes and looks with all one's will to believe – and yet it everywhere reaches way

beyond them (only a god could till such a field of vision) – there stands a vase column, a single survivor, and one cannot comprehend it, only in combination with the night can one grasp it somehow..."

[154] Br. 410.

[155] Butler pp 391f.

[156] T. T. p. 149. "Actually I should like to be at home a great deal. The visitors have taken over, and woe betide if one crosses St. Mark's in the evening and finds them all lit up by the glow-lamps of the illumination; this stupid superlative of light drives the last features from their faces, they all look ah-ah-ah, without differentiation or gradation; I don't know how they distinguish one another in this condition; probably by way of the waiter at whose table they are sitting".

[157] Geering p. 95.

[158] Leisi p. 224 "Destiny, a frequently used term, signifies in the late Rilke, a principle inimical to Orpheus". "In the sonnets destiny always appears as an opponent to Orpheus".

[159] *Briefe aus Muzot* p. 18. "I call destiny all those outward events (including sicknesses, for example) which can inevitably come to interrupt and destroy a spiritual disposition and formation that is by nature solitary".

[160] v. Salis p. 229. "Never forget, dear one, life is glorious!"

[161] S. W. 2, 115. "Danger has become more secure than security".

[162] S. W. 2, 368f. Leishman translates *op. cit.* pp 114f: "Lord, be not good: be glorious; gainsay / that hearsay of you they are all extolling: / unroof the house, the bridge unstay, / and set a swarm of violence rolling / along the fugitive's by-way. // For we are so enslaved to small privation, / it's now the universal view / that if two hands reached out in sustenation / a god were there. Red night of tribulation, / you fire-glow, you warfare, you starvation: / slay, for our only peril's you. // Not till we've once again transferred to you / our perishing as well as our upbearing / will all be yours: both loneliness and pairing, / the going under and the coming through. / To rouse in us what you at last can still, / you must set on to us and lacerate us; / for nothing can enough annihilate us / to the requirements of your saving will".

[163] S. W. 2, 457f. Leishman translates *op. cit.* p. 250: "Not that

it's harmless. The petty and prettifying error / that be-aprons it
and be-frills only deceived for a time. / It is no more certain than
we and never more shielded; / no god can counterbalance its
weight. Defenceless / as we ourselves, defenceless as beasts in
winter. / More defenceless – no hiding places. Defenceless / as
though itself were the thing that threatened. Defenceless / as fire,
giants, poison, as goings-on / at night in suspected houses with
bolted doors // For who can fail to see that the guardian hands /
lie, while trying to defend it, – themselves in danger ... Yet, /
what you've described is peril itself, the entire / pure
perilousness of the world, – and thus it turns to protection, / soon
as you feel it completely. The fervour of childhood / stands like a
centre within it: *out*-fearing it, fearless".

[164] S. W. 2, 291.
[165] S. W. 2, 290f.
[166] 5 January 1910. Br. 115.
[167] S. W. 2, 210.
[168] S. W. 1, 654.
[169] S. W. 1, 170f.
[170] S. W. 2, 435f. Leishman translates *op. cit.* pp 215f.: "You've
all at once, you summer's imitator, / updrawn my seed into a
sudden tree. / (Feel in yourself, so spacious inwardly, / the over-
arching night, its consummator.) / It rose, and to the firmament
would reach, / a risen reflection, imitating trees. / Oh, fell it, that,
inverted, it may go / into your womb and ultimately know / that
counter-heaven to which it's really surging. / Bold landscape,
such as gazers will begin / to see in crystals. That Within / to
which the stars' outsideness is converging".
[171] S. W. 2, 167f. Leishman translates *op. cit.* p. 310: "The ones
birds plunge through's not the intimate space / where each
confided form's intensified. / (Out in the open there you're self-
denied, / and go on vanishing without a trace.) // Space spreads
transposingly from us to things: / really to feel the way a tree
upsprings. / cast round it space from that which inwardly /
expands in you. Surround it with retention. / It has no bounds.
Not till its reascension / in your renouncing is it truly tree".
[172] S. W. 2, 394.
[173] von Salis p. 228.
[174] S. W. 2, 511.

175 S. W. 2, 466. Leishman translates *op. cit.* p. 264: "Seek no
more than what the Attic stela / and its gently-chiselled image
know: / almost cheerfully, as though they feel a / lightening of
what here perplexes so. // Be content to feel the pure direction /
in the river that returns no more …"

176 S. W. 2, 488f. Leishman translates *op. cit.* p. 311: "In such a
clinging pattern interfused / into this goat-wool's delicate
enfolding: / sheer happiness, that never can be used, / purely
surrendered to this wonder-holding // web into which life took
that sudden spring. / What motion finds survival in the pure /
existence and persistence of a thing!"

177 von Salis pp 209f. "If I should succumb to a serious
illness, which led in the end to mental disturbance, I ask, indeed
implore my friends to keep far away from me any priestly
presence that might try to intrude on me. Bad enough that, in my
physical distress, I should have to admit a mediator and manager
in the person of the doctor; every spiritual middleman would be
insulting and repugnant to the movement of my soul, directed as
it is towards the open".

178 von Salis p. 229. " Help me to *my own* death. I do not want
the death of the doctors. I want my freedom".

179 8 November 1915. Br. 247. "Could one not treat the history
of God as, as it were, a region of the human soul not yet entered
into, something always postponed, saved up and in the end
neglected, lost ..."

180 S. W. 2, 468.

181 10 March 1922. Br. 355.

182 25 Januay 1921. Br. 312.

183 S. W. 3, 207.

184 S. W. 2, 101f. Leishman translates *op. cit.* pp 213f.: "Alas,
my mother will demolish me! / Stone after stone upon myself I'd
lay, / and stood already like a little house round which the day /
rolls boundlessly. / Now mother's coming to demolish me: //
demolish me by simply being there. / That building's going on
she's unaware. / Through my stone wall she passes heedlessly. /
Alas, my mother will demolish me! / In lighter flight the birds
encircle me. / The strange dogs know already: this is *he*. / It's
hidden only from my mother's glance, / my gradually
augmented countenance. // No warm wind ever blew to me from

her. / She's not at home where breezes are astir. / In some heart-attic she is tucked away, / and Christ comes there to wash her every day".

[185] Letter to R. v. Kühlmann, quoted by Mörchen p. 373.

[186] to Ilse Jahr 22 February 1923. Br. 379. "Now you would hardly ever hear me name Him, there is an indescribable discretion between us, and where once was proximity and penetration new distances extend ... the tangible eludes, becomes transformed, instead of possession one learns relationship and there arises a namelessness that must begin again with God in order to be perfect and without subterfuge ... the attributes are taken from God, the no longer sayable, and returned to creation, to love and death ... and all that is profound and fervent in the here and now, which the Church had misappropriated in favour of the other world, comes back again; all the angels commit themselves, sing their praises, to the earth".

[187] 8 November 1915. Br. 247. "God and Death were now outside, were the Other, whereas this here was our life, which now, at the cost of this exclusion, seemed to be human, familiar, possible, achievable, in a closed sense ours ... if a tree blossoms, death blossoms in it just as much as life, and the ploughed field is full of death, which puts forth from its prone countenance a rich expression of life, and the animals move patiently from one to the other – and everywhere around us death is still at home and looks out on us from the cracks in things, and a rusty nail, standing out somewhere from a plank of wood, does nothing day and night but rejoice over it". "His enormous nature-experience (I know hardly anyone else so passionately embedded in nature) enabled him to an astonishing degree to think and to write out of the whole, out of a life-feeling that was so saturated with such finely distributed death that it seemed to be present everywhere as a singular spice in the strong taste of life – but for that very reason could this same man be so alarmed and aghast, when he became aware that somewhere there was mere death, the flask full of death or the ugly cup with the broken handle and the senseless inscription 'Faith, Charity, Hope', from which one was compelled to drink the bitterness of an undiluted death".

[188] S. W. 2, 104f. Letter of 14 January 1919.Br. 277. Leishman

translates *op. cit.* p. 218: "There, a blue draught for somebody to drain, / stands Death, in a large cup without a saucer. / A rather odd position for a cup: / stands on the back of a hand. And still quite plain / and visible along the smooth glazed slope / the place where the handle snapped. Dusty. And "Hope" / inscribed in letters half washed down the sink. // The drinker destinated for the drink / spelt them at breakfast in some distant past. // What kind of creatures these are, that at last / have to be poisoned off, it's hard to think. // Else, would they stay? Has this hard food, in fact, / such power to infatuate, / they'd eat for ever, did not some hand extract / the crusty present, like a dental plate? // Which leaves them babbling. Bab, bab, ba ... /// O falling star, / seen from a bridge once in a foreign land: – / remembering you, to stand!"

[189] S. W. 2,318f.

[190] S. W. 2,261.Leishman translates *op. cit.* p. 309: "As Nature lets the other creatures follow / the daring of their dim delight, alone, / giving no special heed to hill or hollow,– / we, too, are no whit dearer to our own / background of being; *it dares us*. Though, at least, / more daringly than plant or beast, / we will this daring, walk with it, and woo it, / and sometimes (in no self-regarding sense) dare against Life itself and just outdo it ... / And this secures us where we've no defence / and feel the pull of elemental force. / Defencelessness! Our last and best resource! / We turned you inside out us when we saw / the world outside grow menacing, and waited / till we could re-affirm it, reinstated / in some wide orbit of recovered law".

[191] S. W. 1,773.

[192] S. W. 2, 158, 160.

[193] Betz pp 176ff.

[194] Mörchen pp 398ff., 486f.

[195] S. W. 1,773. Leisi's contention (p.172) that the friend addressed is Orpheus is unlikely. More convincing is the suggestion of the K.A. editors, who link the sonnet directly with the preceding one, so that here Vera is addressing the poet. (p. 763)

[196] Letter to Countess Dietrichstein 26 June 1917. Br. 257. "rings out time and destiny over the lake, as though it included in itself the visibility of all the lives that have been surrendered here; as though again and again it were sending their

transitoriness into space, invisibly, in the sonorous
transformation of its notes".

[197] T. T. 2, 893. "This soul takes everything upon itself. It commends the wide-openness of the heart ... It is a naive, aeolian soul, which is not ashamed to dwell where the senses intersect, and which wants for nothing, since those unfolded senses form a circle which has no break; so it rests in the consciousness of an uninterrupted world".

[198] Caspar Barth, *Deutscher Phönix*.

[199] K. A. 2, p. 717.

[200] *Lettres françaises à Merline*, pp 18f.

[201] Letter to Marianne von Goldschmidt-Rothschild, 5 December 1914. Br. 226.

[202] *Rilke / Zwetajewa*, esp. pp 7, 28, 35, 37.

[203] S. W. 1, 271ff.

BIBLIOGRAPHY OF WORKS CITED

RILKE'S WORKS, LETTERS, TRANSLATIONS:

Rainer Maria Rilke, *Sämtliche Werke*. (Rilke-Archiv edition). 6 vols. Frankfurt am Main: 1955–1966. [=S.W.]

Rilke, *Werke. Kommentierte Ausgabe*. 4 vols. (eds.) Manfred Engel, Ulrich Fülleborn, Horst Nalewski, August Stahl. Frankfurt am Main/Leipzig: 1996. [=K.A.]

Das Florenzer Tagebuch. Frankfurt: 1942.

Tagebücher aus der Frühzeit. Leipzig: 1942.

Rainer Maria Rilke. *Briefe*. (Rilke-Archiv Edition). 2 vols. Wiesbaden: 1950. [=Br.]

Rainer Maria Rilke und Marie von Thurn und Taxis. *Briefwechsel*. (ed.) Ernst Zinn, 2 vols. Zürich: 1951. [T.T.]

Rainer Maria Rilke. *Briefe an seinen Verleger*. 2 vols., (ed.) Ruth Sieber-Rilke and Carl Sieber. Wiesbaden: 1949. [=B.V.]

Rainer Maria Rilke / Katharina Kippenberg, *Briefwechsel*, Wiesbaden: 1954. [=KK]

Rainer Maria Rilke – Lou Andreas-Salomé, *Briefwechsel*, (ed.) Ernst Pfeiffer. Zürich/Wiesbaden 1952. [Br.A-S.]

Rainer Maria Rilke, *Die Briefe an Frau Gudi Nölke*, (ed.) Paul Obermüller, Wiesbaden: 1953. [=GN]

Briefe aus den Jahren 1902–1906, (ed.) Ruth Sieber-Rilke and Carl Sieber. Leipzig: 1929.

Briefe an Sidonie Nádherny von Borutin. Frankfurt: 1973.

Briefe aus Muzot 1921 bis 1926. Leipzig: 1937.

Lettres françaises à Merline 1919–1922. Paris: 1950.

Briefe an Nanny Wunderly-Volkart, 2 vols. Frankfurt: 1977. (Br. W-V)

Die Briefe an Frau Gudi Nölke. Wiesbaden: 1953.

Rainer Maria Rilke's Duineser Elegien, (ed.) E. L. Stahl. Oxford: 1965.

Rainer Maria Rilke. *Duino Elegies.* The German text with an English translation, introduction and commentary by J. B. Leishman and Stephen Spender. London: 1948.

Rainer Maria Rilke *Sonnets to Orpheus.* The German text, with an English translation, introduction and notes by J. B. Leishman. London: 1946.

Rainer Maria Rilke. The *Sonnets to Orpheus.* Translated by Stephen Mitchell. Boston: 1993.

Rainer Maria Rilke. *Duino Elegies* and *The Sonnets to Orpheus.* Translated by A. Poulin, Jr. Boston 1977.

Duineser Elegien / Die Sonette an Orpheus. Les Elégies de Duino / Les Sonnets à Orphée. Traduits et préfacés. J.-F. Angelloz. (Aubier, Editions Montaigne) 1943.

Rainer Maria Rilke. *Poems 1906 to 1926.* Translated with an Introduction by J. B. Leishman. Norfolk, Connecticut: 1957.

Rainer Maria Rilke. *Sonnets to Orpheus.* Translated by M. D. Herter. Norton. New York: 1992.

Rainer Maria Rilke. *The Sonnets to Orpheus*. Translated by Leslie Norris and Alan Keele. London: 1991.

Rainer Maria Rilke. *Sonnets to Orpheus*. Translated by David Young. Hanover, New Hampshire: 1988.

Sonnets to Orpheus by Rainer Maria Rilke. Translated by Charles Haseloff. Privately printed at the Print Center, Brooklyn: 1979.

Rilke's *Sonnets to Orpheus*. Translated by C. F. MacIntyre. Berkeley/Los Angeles: 1960.

Rilke, *Selected Poems*. Translated by J. B. Leishman. London: 1964.

Rainer Maria Rilke *Prose and Poetry*, (ed.) Egon Schwarz. New York: 1991.

Rilke Between Roots. Selected Poems Rendered from the German by Rika Lesser. Princeton University Press: 1986.

An Unofficial Rilke Poems 1912–1926. Selected, translated and with an introduction by Michael Hamburger. London: 1981.

The Selected Poetry of Rainer Maria Rilke. Edited and translated by Stephen Mitchell. London: 1987.

The Best of Rilke. Translated by Walter Arndt. Hanover/London: 1989.

Poems from the Book of Hours. Translated by Babette Deutsch. London: 1947.

The Book of Hours. Translated by A. L. Peck. London: 1961.

WORKS ON RILKE

Albert-Lasard, Lou: *Wege mit Rilke*. Frankfurt: 1952.

Andreas-Salomé, Lou: *Rainer Maria Rilke*. Leipzig: 1928.

Bassermann, Dieter: *Der späte Rilke*. Essen and Freiburg 1. Br.:1948.

Bassermann, Dieter: *Der andere Rilke*. Bad Homburg: 1961.

Berendt, Hans: *Rainer Maria Rilkes Neue Gedichte*. Bonn: 1957.

Betz, Maurice: *Rilke in Paris*. Zurich: 1948.

Bolinow. Otto Friedrich: *Rilke*. Stuttgart: 1951.

Buddeberg, Else: *Die Duineser Elegien R. M Rilkes*. Karlsruhe: 1948.

Buddeberg, Else: 'Orpheus. Eurydike. Hermes', in *Die Deutsche Lyrik. Von der Spätromantik bis zur Gegenwart,* ed. Benno von Wiese. Düsseldorf: 1956. pp.318-335.

Butler, E. M.: *Rainer Maria Rilke*. Cambridge: 1941.

Casey, T. J.: *Rainer Maria Rilke. A Centenary Essay*. London: 1976.

Geering, Agnes: *Rainer Maria Rilkes Sonette an Orpheus*. Frankfurt am Main: 1948.

Guardini Romano: *Rainer Maria Rilkes Deutung des Daseins*. München: 1953.

Hähnel, Klaus-Dieter: *Rainer Maria Rilke. Werk - Literaturgeschichte – Kunstanschauung.* Berlin – Weimar: 1984.

Hattingberg, Magda von: *Rilke und Benvenuta.* Wien: 1947.

Holthusen, H. F.: *Rainer Maria Rilke. A Study of his Later Poetry.* Translated by J. P. Stern. Cambridge: 1952.

Jaloux, Edmond: *La Dernière Amitié de R. M. Rilke.* Paris: 1949.

Kippenberg, Katharina: *Rainer Maria Rilke. Ein Beitrag.* Leipzig: 1942.

Kippenberg, Katharina: *R.M.Rilkes Duineser Elegien und Sonette an Orpheus.* Wiesbaden: 1948.

Kohlschmidt, Werner: *R. M. Rilke.* Lübeck: 1948.

Kretschmar, Eberhard: *Die Weisheit R. M. Rilkes.* Weimar: 1963.

Leisi, Ernst: *Rilkes Sonette an Orpheus.* Tübingen: 1987.

Leppmann, Wolfgang: *Rilke. Leben und Werk.* Bern: 1981.

Mason, Eudo C.: *Rilke.* Edinburgh: 1963.

Mason, Eudo C.: *Lebenshaltung und Symbolik bei Rainer Maria Rilke.* Oxford: 1964.

Mason, Eudo C.: *Rainer Maria Rilke. Sein Leben und sein Werk.* Göttingen: 1964.

Mason, Eudo C.: *Exzentrische Bahnen.* Göttingen: 1963.

Mörchen, Hermann: *Rilkes Sonette an Orpheus.* Stuttgart: 1958.

Prater, Donald: *A Ringing Glass. The Life of Rainer Maria Rilke.* Oxford: 1986.

Rehm, Walther: Orpheus. Der Dichter und die Toten. Düsseldorf: 1950.

Salis, J. R. von: *Rainer Maria Rilkes Schweizerjahre.* Frauenfeld: 1952.

Schmidt-Paul, Elisabeth v.: *Rainer Maria Rilke. Ein Gedenkbuch.* Stuttgart: 1946.

Schnack, Ingeborg: *Rilke Chronik.* Frankfurt: 1996.

Schwarz, Egon: *Das verschluckte Schluchzen: Poesie und Politik bei Rainer Maria Rilke.* Frankfurt: 1972.

Sieber, Carl: *René Rilke. Die Jugend Rainer Maria Rilkes.* Leipzig: n.d.

Stahl, August: *Rilke-Kommentar zum Lyrischen Werk.* München: 1978.

Steiner, Jacob: *Rilkes Duineser Elegien.* Bern: 1962.

Thurn und Taxis-Hohenlohe, Fürstin Marie von: *Erinnerungen an Rainer Maria Rilke.* München/Berlin: 1933.

Wolff, Joachim: *Rilkes Grabschrift.* Heidelberg: 1983.